My Saigon: The Local Guide to Ho Chi Minh City, Vietnam

My Saigon, Volume 1

Elly Thuy Nguyen

Published by Elly Thuy Nguyen, 2024.

While every precaution has been taken in the preparation of this book, the publisher assumes no responsibility for errors or omissions, or for damages resulting from the use of the information contained herein.

MY SAIGON: THE LOCAL GUIDE TO HO CHI MINH CITY, VIETNAM

First edition. January 21, 2024.

Copyright © 2024 Elly Thuy Nguyen.

ISBN: 978-1484929117

Written by Elly Thuy Nguyen.

Table of Contents

Introduction to the 2024 edition 1
Saigon or Ho Chi Minh City? 3
Spelling and pronunciation 7
Should I visit Hanoi or Saigon? 9
Saigon Geography: Qs, Ps, and maps 11
Airport arrivals and Saigonese history 17
Vietnam visas and practical airport tips 21
Transportation into the city 31
Internet and SIM cards 35
Grab: the app you need 41
Shopping: the magic of grocery stores 45
Tip-top tipping tips 47
Street safety and crime in Saigon 49
Women's safety 55
Covid precautions and masks 57
Vietnamese language reference 61
"You you you!" 77
"Motorbike!" 79
You called me what? 81
The Saigon no 83
Where to stay? 85
Dollars and dong 91
Getting around 97
Eating (way beyond pho) 101
Ngon and other tourist trap restaurants 105
Best pho in Saigon 109
Will they secretly serve you dog meat? 113
A warning about food allergies 115
What's a typical Saigonese meal? 117

- Chuyen Ky: traditional Saigonese food 121
- Saigonese breakfast on a hot plate....................................123
- Where to hang out in Saigon? 129
- How to score chicks in Vietnam 135
- Gay Saigon 143
- Who are those young women in tight clothes?..............147
- The wacky tobacky 149
- Where to hang out in cafes..151
- Date street: Phan Xich Long..157
- Late-night Saigon 161
- Ben Thanh Market, local style 167
- Walking Ban Co Market 173
- Cat cafe 177
- Five floors of hipsters for a rainy day 179
- Four ultra-hipster cafes..181
- Four Saigon street food streets.......................................185
- Saigon screams for ice cream 189
- Chinatown alley for your Insta 195
- Egg coffee and a river walk...199
- No turtles, no lake, but a great evening hangout............201
- A walk in the park 205
- Neighborhood Buddhist temple 209
- Saigon's Cao Dai temple: uniquely Vietnamese.............213
- Hair wash 215
- Vietnamese green bean cakes 217
- Where to meet university students.................................219
- Where to listen to live music...221
- Nhau (getting drunk)...225
- A Vietnamese massage you might not enjoy..................227
- Moshi moshi, Japantown 231
- Clothes shopping..233

Don't overpay for luggage 235
Medical tourism 237
Taxi scams..243
Shady business scams 247
Broken phone or laptop? Fret not! 249
Don't wear that silly hat: cultural tips 251
Elly's public service announcement 255
Send-off 259

Introduction to the 2024 edition

This book is an in-depth local guide to Saigon, otherwise known as Ho Chi Minh City, Vietnam.

Saigon is a thrill of a city: a richly textured, many-layered megalopolis combining a huge range of historical periods, cultures, ideologies, social strata, attitudes, and activities.

Yet Saigon is unappreciated, or underappreciated, by tourist guidebooks and tourists alike: the good stuff rarely appears in guidebooks, and the good places rarely have any foreign visitors. The best of Saigon is in Saigonese people's conversations and recommendations, and very rarely in books or websites.

This book brings that knowledge to visitors, or anyone curious about this city.

I omit the standard items about the Opera Building and other usual Saigon tourist attractions, because a million books and websites already talk about those things.

Instead, I've made this book a locals' guide, detailing where Saigonese people would go with their friends if they had a free day in the city – which is not where the tourist guidebooks would send you.

Using this book, a visitor can experience Saigon as an in-the-know local Saigonese person would, with a deeper understanding of the city and its environment, and a range of experiences normally outside visitors' ken. These are the recommendations, the tips, and the advice I'd give a friend or relative visiting Saigon. It's very different from where standard mass-market guidebooks tell you to go.

Standard guidebooks to Saigon generally fall into two categories: written by a non-Vietnamese person, or full of undisclosed advertising. Either way, the reader doesn't get the best of Saigon. *My Saigon* changed all that when it first came out in 2013, and it's still bringing it, eleven years later.

This is the 2024 edition. Same Elly quality, same Elly jokes, but added new places, removed closed-down places, updated visa information, got with the times on transport and internet, and all the other usual updates you'd expect. I've also included a discussion and instructions for the new 90-day multiple-entry electronic visas Vietnam started issuing on August 15, 2023.

Leave the tourists to their tourist traps. Let them wear their conical hats. Enjoy the local thrills. You'll love it. I promise.

Saigon or Ho Chi Minh City?

Foreign visitors often ask: *What is the difference between Saigon and Ho Chi Minh City?*

The short answer is that the difference is historical and ideological. Ho Chi Minh City is the government-mandated new name of the city, post-1975. Many people in Saigon, and throughout Vietnam, continue to use the old name, because reasons. You know. *Reasons*.

Which name a Vietnamese person uses for the city is a pretty strong statement of their regional and cultural identity. Regional rifts in Vietnam are much older than the 1960s-1975 war, and they certainly didn't go away in 1975.

The long answer? In the 1600s, this city was called "Gia Dinh" (pronounced "za din" or "ya din," depending on what region you're from; see note below about regional pronunciation), originally a Chinese word, as Vietnam had been a vassal of China for a thousand years. In the 1800s, when the French colonized Vietnam, they Westernized "za din" to the word "Saigon."

As you probably know, Vietnam fought a civil war from the 1960s until 1975. North Vietnam (supported by the USSR and China) fought against South Vietnam (supported by the US, South Korea, Australia, and other countries that weren't the USSR and China). North Vietnam won the war on April 30, 1975 and took over South Vietnam.

Soon after taking over South Vietnam, the North Vietnamese leaders provisionally renamed Saigon to Ho Chi Minh City. In 1977, the name change was made official and permanent. The city had been the capital of South Vietnam, but after the war, South Vietnam no longer existed, and Hanoi became the capital of the newly unified (on maps, anyway) nation of Vietnam.

In Vietnamese, the word for "city" is "thanh pho," so you will sometimes see references to "Thanh Pho Ho Chi Minh" or "TP Ho Chi Minh" or "TP HCM" or similar. The "TP" or "thanh pho" just means "city."

Although the official name is Thanh Pho Ho Chi Minh, most local people still call this city Saigon. Some people – especially those who emigrated to the United States – make a point of saying "Saigon" instead of "Ho Chi Minh City," in order to make a political statement. Other people are just accustomed to the older name. It's shorter. Still, some other people do say "Ho Chi Minh City," especially those born after the war, and those from the northern areas that were North Vietnam, where the name "Saigon" is still in disfavor.

In the years immediately after the war, the name "Saigon" was forbidden to use throughout Vietnam. But nowadays, even government travel guides refer to the city as "Saigon." The government company that owns some hotels is called SaigonTourist. So now the word "Saigon" has maybe lost its strong political flavor and can be used neutrally even by the Vietnamese government.

To make things a bit more complicated, some older Saigonese people say *Saigon* to mean the central area of the city, and *Ho Chi Minh* to mean the outer districts. That's because while the renaming got all the attention, simultaneously with being renamed, the city was also expanded. What had previously been suburban villages outside Saigon were

MY SAIGON: THE LOCAL GUIDE TO HO CHI MINH CITY, VIETNAM

incorporated into the larger Ho Chi Minh City. That sort of distinction is really mostly common among older Saigonese people, say above sixty: those who remember the old borders of Saigon.

People who weren't born yet in 1975, or at least weren't old enough to read maps back then, are more likely to say *Saigon* to refer to the entirety of Ho Chi Minh City, including the outer districts that originally weren't part of Saigon.

And to be perfectly honest, many Vietnamese people just don't care what you call this city. Worrying about by what names we call cities is a bit of a luxury, isn't it? Many people in Vietnam, even in Saigon, are too worried about getting their next meal to care about whether we say *Saigon* or *Ho Chi Minh*.

Anyway.

In this book, I will say *Saigon*. I wasn't born before the war. And I'm not making a political statement (or am I?). But *Saigon* is easier to say and write, and it's usually what my friends and I call this city. So, if you were talking to me in person, I'd say *Saigon*. And when you're reading this book, I'll also say *Saigon*.

Spelling and pronunciation

The Vietnamese language uses an alphabet very similar to the Roman alphabet. That's thanks to a group of Vietnamese scholars building on the work of a French missionary, Alexandre de Rhodes. (There's a street named after Alexandre de Rhodes in central Saigon – one of the very few streets with Western names that were not renamed after 1975.)

Until the early 20th century, Vietnamese was usually written using Chinese characters, a writing system called *chu nom*. The Romanized alphabet was invented in the late 1800s, but was adopted only slowly and hesitantly, but by the 1940s, the Romanized alphabet had taken hold. It was declared the official alphabet when Vietnam won independence from France.

The alphabet being Romanized means that you, as presumably a Roman alphabet user, can make some sense of signs, menus, and written stuff in general. But the Vietnamese alphabet is not completely Romanized, because in Vietnam we have those marks on the letters – the marks are called diacritics. We also have two types of letter D, one with a horizontal line through it, and one without. If you were studying or using the Vietnamese language in an intensive and serious way, those marks would make a difference to you.

Because I'm assuming that you are only a visitor to Vietnam, and not a serious student of the Vietnamese language, I am going to make things easier on your reading device, and not use those special Vietnamese letters in this book – instead using the closest letters in the Roman alphabet.

So you won't see those special marks (diacritics), because most non-Vietnamese electronic book readers can't render them anyway, so I think it's better to go without them instead of having words rendered as "????????" (that is how I saw Vietnamese text rendered on a reader – all question marks!).

When I teach you how to pronounce something, it's going to be the Saigon pronunciation, and using Saigon vocabulary. Hanoians pronounce some letters differently from Saigonese. Most notably, the letter "D" (without the line through it) and the letters "GI" (together) are pronounced in Saigon as *y* as in "yankee" but in Hanoi are pronounced as *z* like in "zebra." So for example, those fried spring rolls that foreign visitors often like to eat are spelled "cha gio" in Vietnamese – in Saigon pronounced as "cha yo," in Hanoi pronounced as "cha zo."

Moreover, the war's winners get to write not just the history books, but also the pronunciation guides. The Northern pronunciation is the official government pronunciation.

Often an official guidebook or phrasebook will teach the Northern pronunciation, and not mention the Southern pronunciation. So you might think that the pronunciation I'm teaching you here is "wrong." Well, it's how everyone in Saigon pronounces words. Foreign tourists get a lot of leeway and people will appreciate you trying to pronounce Vietnamese no matter how you try to do it, but if you're going to attempt it in Saigon, then I'm going to be teaching you the Saigon pronunciation, so you can fit in better. This is a local's guide to Saigon, right?

Should I visit Hanoi or Saigon?

It depends on what you're interested in. A very short summary: Hanoi has more classical Vietnamese culture and history, while Saigon is a big bustling city. Hanoi is known for small alleys, quiet streets, and people who are best described as "reserved." Saigon is known for wide-open boulevards, commercialism, and people who are described as "open."

I think (as a Saigon girl) that foreigners are treated better in Saigon; you are much more likely to be cheated and otherwise mistreated in Hanoi. Hanoi has a long history of being an isolated place with no foreigners (aside from Russian "advisors"), unlike Saigon, which was intimately associated with Western countries until the 1975 changes.

Customer service is definitely better in Saigon. For historical reasons, Hanoians tend to have a gruff, aggressive, "Soviet Union" attitude to customer service. Saigonese people love to tell stories — maybe sometimes exaggerated — of the time they went to Hanoi and the waiter or shop clerk angrily screamed at them.

Do I sound biased about Hanoi? Well, I'm a Saigon girl. And Hanoians always move to Saigon, but Saigonese people rarely move to Hanoi.

Let's tell a Saigonese joke! "Hanoi is now in Saigon, and Saigon is now in California." Like most jokes, it exaggerates, but does carry a grain of truth.

One thing that you might like about Hanoi is the cooler weather. Saigon can be blisteringly hot. In the winter, Hanoi is cold enough for you to need a good winter coat – too cold for me, but some people like it.

Of course I recommend that you come to Saigon. After all, this book is called *My Saigon*.

About Hanoi – my recommendation is that if you have the free time in your trip to Vietnam, and can spare a few hundred dollars for roundtrip airfare, then you can hop over to Hanoi for a couple of days to check it out, see the historical sights, and so on. You will, as a foreign tourist, generally be treated worse in Hanoi than in Saigon, but who cares about *generally*? You can still have amazing experiences, wherever you go.

Shameless plug: I wrote a guidebook to Hanoi. It's called *Happy in Hanoi*. Read it or don't read it; either way, you will regret it. (Just kidding.) (I've also published guidebooks to Da Nang, Quy Nhon, and Vietnamese women. Seriously.)

Quick tip on traveling between Saigon and Hanoi: Please take Vietnam Airlines, not VietJet (NotYetJet), Bamboo (Bamboozle), or any of the other low-cost carriers. We don't have consumer protections in Vietnam, so the low-cost carriers are terrible to deal with, and they will cancel or delay your flight, or mistreat you in a million other ways, anytime they feel like it. Vietnam Airlines isn't great, but it's better than the alternatives.

Saigon Geography: Qs, Ps, and maps

Saigon is divided into districts, called quans. They're like boroughs in New York City. In an address in Vietnamese, you might see "Quan 1" or "Q1." That means District 1. In English-language addresses you'll see "District 1" or "D1." The words *quan* and *district* are interchangeable.

You might find that Vietnamese people, even those who speak English well, have trouble pronouncing the word *district*. We're not good with grouped consonants! Usually *district* from a Vietnamese person comes out sounding more like *detit*. Hey, just say *quan*!

I'm going to say *quan* in this guidebook, because this is an insiders' guide, and Vietnamese people say *quan,* not *district*.

If you're in Saigon as a tourist, you'll likely spend most of your time in Quan 1. That's the central city, Saigon's Manhattan. Unless you speak Vietnamese, or unless you are here for some very specific reason that's not in Quan 1, you'll probably be best off staying in a hotel in Quan 1. Quan 1 is the center of things.

Here are the quans (districts) you might encounter when seeing the locations of places:

Q 1: Central business district, as we discussed.

Q 3: Very close to the central business district, and almost becoming the same as Q1. This is the quan that you are most likely to visit if you visit a quan outside of Q1.

Dakao: Actually a part of Q 1, but often informally considered its own quan. To make things more confusing,

Dakao is part of Q 1, but is geographically closer to most of Q 3.

Q 4: The hood. Traditionally, the hood, infamous for poverty and street crime. Nowadays it's gotten better. Still, be aware that this is the neighborhood your upper-middle-class Saigonese parents would never let you set foot in. Landlords and hotel owners in Q4 mostly market to foreigners, because among Vietnamese people, Q4 is a notoriously undesirable place. Personally? I don't set foot in Q4. I just don't. But I'm a bit of a stick in the mud and a scaredy cat. I have friends who happily go partying in Q4 and return with all limbs intact.

Q 5 ("Cholon"): "Chinatown," with some great Chinese restaurants. It's probably not at the top of your to-visit list, but don't neglect it completely. You might be especially interested if you can speak Cantonese, the traditional language used in Q 5. Most of the ethnically Chinese residents left in 1975 and the immediately following years, actually, and nowadays, the ethnically Chinese people in Q5 are a minority — but a pretty big minority. (Anyway, the distinction between "Chinese" and "Vietnamese" is a very hazy one, but that's a big topic for another time.)

Q 6 and Q 11: While Q 5 is known as "Chinatown," most of the actual Chinese culture, including the big Chinese market area (Cholon) is actually in the adjoining Q6 and Q11. They're not far from Q 5, and some people even think they're a part of Q 5, but they're not.

Q Phu Nhuan: An area between Q 1 and the airport. Some nice restaurants and cafes there, especially along its well-known hangout street, Phan Xich Long. Phu Nhuan might be the easiest way for tourists to get to "average Saigonese life" outside

MY SAIGON: THE LOCAL GUIDE TO HO CHI MINH CITY, VIETNAM

the central tourist areas. Phu Nhuan is known for having many emigres from Hanoi.

Q 2: It's across the river from Q1, and it used to be a sleepy exurb, but now that there's a tunnel connecting it to Q1, it has become an enclave for foreigners. Mostly white foreigners. You will see more English-language than Vietnamese-language signs in Q2. If you are from an English speaking country and want to feel just like home, Q2 is your best bet. (Formerly, this position was occupied by Q7, but nowadays Q7 is for rich Vietnamese people and for Koreans.)

Q 7: Did I say rich Vietnamese people and Koreans? Pretty much. It's an exurb. It has some big malls and Saigon's best hospital (FV Hospital). And Koreans. Lots of Koreans. Get your boy band on. Chincha.

Q Tan Binh: An absolutely huge quan that encompasses the airport and the new exurb developments. You're unlikely to go to Tan Binh, other than for the airport.

Q Binh Thanh: A working-class residential quan near Quan 1, traditionally popular as a bedroom community for blue-collar workers in Q 1. Nowadays, a lot of the Binh Thanh slums have been razed and replaced by high-rise condo buildings, mostly rented out on Airbnb. If you're looking at Airbnb high-rise condos, chances are they're in Binh Thanh. And the absolutely huge Vinhomes/Vinpearl/Vinwhatever development is in Binh Thanh, on the site of some razed slums.

That's really it as far as quans you're likely to visit. Of course there are other quans, and of course there are many worthwhile things in them. But unless you're very adventurous, or unless you can speak Vietnamese or have a Vietnamese-speaking companion who can take you, I don't think there's much reason for you to go there.

There's a Saigonese saying: "Sleep in Q3, work in Q1, eat in Q5, steal in Q4." That sums it up well. Q3 is the most desirable residential area. Q1 is the center of business and nightlife (Vietnamese slang: "di choi," going out to have a good time). Q5 is known for many restaurants, especially Chinese restaurants. And Q4, just across the river from Q1, is, unfortunately, the hood, known for drug addicts and crime, although there is gentrification in progress, and nowadays many foreigners happily live in Q4 and don't know that ten years ago Saigonese people considered Q4 a no-go zone.

Each quan has its own character. And the numbers don't really mean anything as far as which is more centrally located than the other. For example, Q3 is more centrally located than Q2, and Q10 is more central than Q4. Technically speaking, the quan numbers are supposed to go in spiral sequence, like Parisian arrondissements, and you can kind of sort of vaguely see that pattern if you look at a map.

I mentioned Ps and Qs. What are Ps? Each quan is divided into several sub-quans. A sub-quan is called a phuong. Each quan is made of several phuongs. In Vietnamese addresses, phuong is usually abbreviated as p or ph or f. (Strictly speaking, there is no *f* in the Vietnamese alphabet, but we make exceptions sometimes!) So you might see an address like 123 Duong Something, Q 1, p 5. That means the street address is 123, and it's in phuong 5, inside quan 1. And a phuong is usually translated in English as "ward" – which is really strange, because I think of "ward" as a hospital ward or a prison ward — but anyway, if you see something like "123 Something Street,

MY SAIGON: THE LOCAL GUIDE TO HO CHI MINH CITY, VIETNAM

District 1, Ward 1," you'll know that District is Quan and Ward means Phuong.

Vietnamese people often skip the phuong in an address. We don't really care about them. They are very small and even Vietnamese people often don't know or care which phuong they live in. In American terms, consider the phuong the extra four digits after your "regular" zip code. (Yes, I've spent time in the US.)

By the way: when writing or saying your address for taxi drivers, don't use the English words *district* and especially *ward*. Unless the taxi driver is experienced with tourists, he (or she!) will have no idea what *district* and *ward* are. You have to say *quan* and *phuong*. The correct pronunciation of *quan* in Vietnamese sounds like *goowan* in English. The *Q* sound is not like the *q* in *quickly*. It's more like a *g* sound.

For extra credit: *Duong* means road or street. That's why every street sign in Saigon says *Duong* before the actual name of the street. I've heard of foreigners giving an address as "I think it's on Duong street!" Oops!

Google Maps is excellent in Saigon. At least now it is. Previous editions of this book kvetched (isn't that a great English word?) about the failings of Google Maps for Vietnamese addresses, but nowadays it does great. You can confidently use it for both walking and motor transport. You can even use it for public transportation.

The only thing to watch out for with Google Maps in Saigon: while addresses are always solidly correct, sometimes business establishments' listings will be hijacked by fake or competing establishments. So for example you will select Starbucks Quan 5 in Google Maps, and thanks to some shady person working on behalf of a competing coffee shop, you will actually be directed to some other coffee shop, whose address has been spammed into the listing for Starbucks. Just be careful and double-check the authenticity of businesses you find on Google Maps, either with other sources, or when you've reached your destination.

Airport arrivals and Saigonese history

When you arrive at Tan Son Nhat International Airport (SGN), you will be treated to an introductory course on Saigon.

You'll see that the airport terminal is sparkling clean and not too old, probably cleaner and newer than most US airport terminals. But take a look in the bathrooms, or in the employees' rooms, and you'll see something that looks more like the third world. That's what a lot of Saigon looks like: a mix of first-world and third-world, the well-known saying about "a country in transition."

You'll also see that the immigration area is staffed by a more-or-less army of officers in military-type beige uniforms. But they're polite, relaxed, and somewhat friendly. This is Communism, Vietnamese style. Yes, the Communist Party runs the country. But "Communism" in Vietnam is not, or at least now is not, of the ideological and strict kind you might find in China or North Korea.

When you step out of the airport building and into the area to meet arriving passengers, you will see billboards and ads for fast food places, banks, and other businesses. You will also be approached by Vietnamese people ever being the small-time entrepreneurs – you might be approached by someone offering you a taxi, a hotel, a sim card, a rental car, and a prostitute, maybe as a package deal. (I don't recommend you take any of the offers. Those sim cards are notorious for only working long enough for you to get out of sight.)

And then you'll see something even more interesting and more telling. Tons of people there to meet the arriving passengers!

• • • •

Have you ever seen such a high ratio of meeters to arrivers at any other airport? Probably not. And the reason for it has little to do with Vietnamese culture per se. The real reason has to do with recent Vietnamese history.

Starting in 1975, about two million Vietnamese people (primarily from Saigon and its environs) left Vietnam and went to live abroad. It was the biggest human migration in all recorded history. Ethnically Vietnamese people living outside Vietnam are called *Viet kieu*.

There are now three million ethnically Vietnamese people living outside Vietnam. Practically speaking, almost everyone in Saigon has relatives living abroad, and those relatives are likely bringing over more of their family members to join them.

MY SAIGON: THE LOCAL GUIDE TO HO CHI MINH CITY, VIETNAM

What does that have to do with airport arrivals? Well, most of the people arriving at international airport arrivals in Saigon or not vacationers or business travelers, but overseas ethnically Vietnamese people visiting family, usually after a long period of not having met. Their hordes of relatives come to the airport to meet them, often after not having met for years.

Have you seen the movie *Love Actually*? And remember how it begins at the arrivals area of the London airport? With all the reuniting families? The arrivals area of Saigon airport is like that times a million.

I'm not sure how relevant all this historical storytelling is to you as a tourist, but it's an interesting and meaningful bit of Saigon you can see right at the airport terminal, without needing to go to any museums.

Bonus trivia. The airport is called *Tan Son Nhat*. The last word, *nhat*, is pronounced as *nyut* or *yut*, and it means *first*. There were two Tan Son villages outside Saigon: Tan Son Nhat (Tan Son 1) and Tan Son Nhi (Tan Son 2). The airport was built on the site of the first Tan Son village, Tan Son Nhat.

Vietnam visas and practical airport tips

Unless you're from fine, upstanding countries such as Russia or Belarus, you'll need a visa to enter Vietnam. (Ok, fine, there are some actually fine, upstanding countries on the visa-free list, such as Japan, South Korea, and most of Western Europe.)

On August 15, 2023 Vietnam completely changed its e-visa issuance system — both the procedure and the actual website.

The old e-visa regulations are no longer in effect. The new e-visa regulations, as of August 15, 2023:

1. You apply for a visa online, uploading your photo and a photo of your passport info page. If the visa is issued, you print it out yourself. You shouldn't need to prepare any applications or pay any money when you arrive in Vietnam. In fact, Vietnam no longer even has a landing declaration form.
2. You must **not** be physically in Vietnam when you apply for an e-visa. I don't know how strictly they check this, and whether they monitor your entries and exits versus your visa application date. The e-visa application website does block Vietnamese IP addresses. According to my experiments, it blocks all Southeast Asian IP addresses (ASEAN citizens can enter Vietnam visa-free anyway, I guess). If you get an HTTP error message like "Request rejected" when

you try to pull up the application website, use a VPN or go to a different country. VPNs are illegal in Vietnam, so I did this experiment the hard way. And boy are my arms tired!

3. All nationalities / passports can apply for e-visas. That doesn't mean you'll definitely be accepted. Especially if you're from a "developing" country, please don't book your trip to Vietnam until you have your visa in hand. They definitely screen visa applicants by country. If you're from a "first-world" country, you are pretty much guaranteed a visa, unless you (or your relatives, especially if you're ethnically Vietnamese) had negative run-ins with the Vietnamese government.

4. All e-visas are good for 90 days. The expiration date of the visa is fixed and doesn't change even if you arrive in Vietnam later than you originally planned. You can arrive later (but not earlier) than originally planned, and you can leave earlier (but not later) than originally planned.

5. You can apply for a single-entry visa that costs $25, or a multiple-entry visa that costs $50. You pay online with a credit card. They claim to accept all credit cards, but I have a hunch that only Visa cards work.

6. There's a dropdown language selection box to choose between English and Vietnamese. I suggest you leave that setting set to Vietnamese, and either use your web browser's translation feature, or pull up an English version in another window just as a reference while you fill in the Vietnamese version. The English version

is much buggier than the Vietnamese version. When I try the English version, it doesn't even populate the drop-down boxes, but the Vietnamese version works fine.

The new application has more questions than before, likely to weed out "tourists" defacto living in Vietnam (the questions about your previous stays in Vietnam), criminals (the question about your previous crimes), and people judged economically undesirable (the questions about the costs of your trip, your job, and your insurance). They also want to know the details about your Vietnamese relatives, probably for the Vietnamese police to know what doors to break down if they're looking for you.

Any Vietnam visa instructions you might find online or in a book that mention 30-day e-visas are outdated and referring to the previous visa regulations. And bafflingly, the old visa application website is still up, even though it supposedly is no longer valid.

So make sure you're on the right website. The correct website to apply for a Vietnam visa after August 15, 2023 is:

https://immigration.gov.vn/ and click on *E-visa*.

Welcome to Vietnamese bureaucracy! Enjoy your stay.

For this application, the first thing you'll need to do is verify your email address. Enter your email address and click the button next to it. You'll get a security code in your email. Then you can have fun filling out the rest of the application. Remember to upload a selfie (white background, no eyeglasses, no hat, no smile) and a photo of your passport info page (the page with your name and info, not the cover page!). Each of those uploaded image files has to be under 1MB. How's the

weather in 1991?

MY SAIGON: THE LOCAL GUIDE TO HO CHI MINH CITY, VIETNAM

After you submit this form, you'll be directed to a payment link. Be very meticulous when you enter your payment card info, because if the transaction gets declined, you have to do the entire application all over again, from the very start. Not just the payment, but the entire application. The word on the street is that the only card that works is Visa, and that even though they claim to accept MasterCard and American Express, those always get declined.

If you have success, congratulations! You'll get a confirmation with two codes. You need both of those codes. The first code, your "record number," will look something like G01.100.100.100-123123-12300. The second code, your "update key," will look something like ABC123ABC. You will need the "record number" to check on the status of your application. You will need the "update key" if you need to make changes to your application.

I'm sorry. Dealing with Vietnam's immigration department isn't easy. (Although being a Vietnamese person getting a visa to a first-world country is more difficult. Ask me how I know.)

According to the website, they no longer email notifications when your visa is ready. Except everyone I've talked to says they *do* email you a notification, with a PDF of your visa, when it's ready. You can also keep checking the website. I recommend you start checking three business days after you apply, but usually it takes more like a week or two. If you haven't heard back after a few weeks, I suggest you contact a private company.

Once you've been approved, you should be able to download the PDF and physically print out the visa. The immigration officer in Vietnam (and the airline check-in clerk in your departure country) will want to see the printed hardcopy visa, not just a phone screenshot.

The Vietnam immigration department claims a three-working-day turnaround time for an e-visa. Like many things in Vietnam, that sometimes happens and sometimes doesn't. According to acquaintances, relatives, and online chatter, sometimes it takes a week or two, while other times it's done the same day. And some people never hear back. The point is, don't count on it taking only three days, because you will need that visa in order to board your flight to Vietnam. I strongly suggest you apply a few weeks in advance.

If you need a visa faster than a week or two, or if you want a more customer-friendly experience (of course, at a higher price), I can recommend a company called Vietnam Visa Pro. There are a lot of websites and companies calling themselves Vietnam Visa Pro, but here's the real one (note the **.net** not **.com** domain name):

http://www.vietnamvisapro.net/en/apply-online.html

Vietnam Visa Pro is easier to deal with than the Vietnamese government, and also more expensive. For regular processing, they cost about twenty dollars more per visa. Importantly, Vietnam Visa Pro also has a rush service. They can get you a visa as fast as one hour. No, it won't be cheap. But have you ever heard of getting a US visa in one hour? (Before you answer that, Google *Michael T. Sestak*.)

If you have an e-visa, you don't need physical passport photos, nor an arrival form, nor a customs form when you arrive in Vietnam. You don't need to fill out anything on the plane. You just go straight to the immigration counter. You also should not have to pay anything upon arrival, although

MY SAIGON: THE LOCAL GUIDE TO HO CHI MINH CITY, VIETNAM

ethnically Vietnamese people are still asked for "a small gift for your brother" at the immigration counters. If you're not ethnically Vietnamese, it won't happen. And if you are asked, I suggest you turn them down. Unless you're feeling generous, in which case, $5 or $10 should be plenty.

There is a "fast track arrival service" available from Vietnam Visa Pro, Klook, and other agencies. For about $30 per person, you'll be able to skip the line at Vietnam Immigration. It's up to you whether it's worth it to you. It is true that the passport-checking lines are pretty long these days, maybe 30-60 minutes, and I have a suspicion that's to encourage the "fast track" option. On the other hand, your checked luggage might take 30-60 minutes to arrive (and baggage claim is after the immigration counters) anyway, so you might not save any time by getting fast-tracked at the immigration counter.

Money? I suggest you change $100 or so at the currency exchange counters either in the checked baggage area or immediately outside it. The rates are not great but not terrible (you'll lose maybe 5% of your money as compared to a good exchange in the central city) and it will give you some cash to use until you make it to an actual currency exchange or ATM.

There are ATMs at the airport, but: a) They are hidden away outside the terminal, b) They are often broken or out of cash, c) If they eat your ATM card, which isn't uncommon in Vietnam, you're in big trouble, because there's no bank to retrieve it. My tip for Vietnam is to only use ATMs that are inside or attached to a bank building. If you do want to use the ATMs at the airport, they're at the lower level (arrivals level), at the far left side as you're walking out of the terminal (far right side if you're facing the terminal building).

You may want to buy a data SIM card if you don't already have one, especially if you want to use the Grab app to get a ride into town. The Saigon airport *theoretically* has free wifi, but in my experience, it seldom works. See the subsequent sections on getting online, transportation into town, and Grab for more details.

Please don't interact with any of the touts who come up to you offering you a taxi, and please don't take any of the "official" SaigonTourist taxis waiting at the "official" taxi queue. They are the worst. They have to pay a lot of money to Some People to operate at that "official" taxi queue, and they'll make that money back by overcharging you. You'll get ripped off, although the amount you'll get ripped off for (maybe 500K

MY SAIGON: THE LOCAL GUIDE TO HO CHI MINH CITY, VIETNAM

VND = $22) is still probably less than you'd pay for an honest airport taxi in the first world.

Transportation into the city

You have a few options:

The cheapest option is the public buses. They are available right outside international arrivals, depart every 30 minutes from 6 AM to midnight daily, and cost 20K VND per person for the express bus (#109) or 6K VND per person for the non-express bus (#152).

Buy your ticket on the bus, with VND cash, preferably small bills. Luggage is supposed to be free, but sometimes the bus conductors will charge a big suitcase as an additional "person." Not many tourists use the buses, but the option is available, and I'm not against it, though I don't know if dealing with a public bus is what you want after a long flight and immigration line. The buses stop in central Saigon and of course you have to make your way to your hotel or destination from there. You can find a lot more info if you Google terms like *Bus 109 airport Saigon*. Note: as with all buses in Vietnam, smoking on public transportation is *theoretically* illegal, but many people still smoke, including the driver.

You can take a taxi. Go outside the international terminal, to the left side, and look for a Vinasun brand taxi. It's a white car with a red-and-green company logo. Make sure it says exactly *Vinasun* not "something similar to *Vinasun*." This will be difficult. There aren't many Vinasun taxis at the airport, often none. Vinasun is an honest taxi company and not affiliated with the airport taxi mafia. Honest taxis are, cough cough, *discouraged* from operating at the airport, and usually any Vinasun taxi that comes around to drop off passengers is quickly snapped up by Vietnamese people who want to take it from the airport to the city. Be careful and don't get into a sound-alike scam taxi like *Vinasu* or *Vinataxi* or *Vantaidulich* or *Vina24* or any number of scammer fakes. Airport to city should cost you 200K max (usually more like 130K), plus 10K for airport parking. (Some drivers want you to pay 20K instead of 10K, to also cover their airport entry fee, which was probably paid by their previous passenger. Whatever. 10K VND is forty US cents. Don't stress about it.) You can tip the driver 10K-50K if he (or she!) helped you with your bags.

If you want a taxi and can't find an honest taxi at the international terminal, walk to the domestic terminal (follow the signs, maybe a five-minute walk outside) and get a Vinasun taxi there. You're more likely to get a Vinasun taxi there, as the domestic terminal isn't as tightly in the grip of the taxi mafia as the international terminal is.

I think the best option is to use Grab, the usual ride app we use in Vietnam. It's basically a very primitive version of Uber. To use Grab, you will need to have downloaded the Grab app. You can set up an account when you're outside Vietnam if you login using Google and have them verify your non-Vietnamese cellphone number over WhatsApp. You can pay for rides in cash, or set up a credit card.

A Grab car costs about 120K-150K from the airport to the city. The driver is supposed to enter the 10K parking toll into the app, but sometimes he might just ask for it from you directly. Other than the 10K for parking, don't pay any more than the app says. And no matter what your driver says, there's no surcharge for night travel, for luggage, or for extra people — the charge in the app is what you pay (other than airport parking). There's no Uber or Lyft in Vietnam. We have a few other ride-hailing apps, such as Be and Gojek, but the drivers never show up and I don't recommend those other apps.

Note that Grab car pickup is in the outdoor parking lot, by a sign that says Grab. The road closer to the terminal is only for personal car pickups. Of course, many Grab drivers don't follow this rule, so look for your driver on the road too. You can use the Grab app to send your driver a photo of yourself and your location.

You can also have your hotel pick you up. I don't recommend this option. First, what hotels charge for airport pickup is generally more expensive than the worst scammer taxis. So you're getting a hotel airport pickup to avoid being scammed at the airport, but you're actually paying more than you would've paid the scammers. As far as I know, hotels charge around 500K for airport pickup, which is on the high side of what scam taxis charge (around 300K-500K usually for a scam taxi). Second, hotels are notorious for not showing up for these airport pickups, then blaming it on you and still sticking you with the bill.

Lastly, if you're absolutely out of your mind and also very courageous, do what I see some foreign tourists doing: walk fifteen minutes to get out of the airport and onto the main road, and wave down a Vinasun taxi there on the main road. This is insane and I don't recommend it, but I'm including it for completeness, because I think it's hilarious. Actually, if you're this hardcore, you might as well walk from the airport to the center of the city. It's only about five miles (8 km), but there aren't any real sidewalks, so please don't actually try to do this.

No, there's no public transportation into the city other than those airport buses. No, the subway that was supposed to have been finished eleven years ago hasn't been built.

Internet and SIM cards

Like to be online? Everywhere in Saigon has free wifi. Seriously, everywhere, including even the smallest hotel. Even streetside restaurants. Even dentists' offices. Even gas stations. In general, we Vietnamese people are very much "online" oriented, perhaps more so than anywhere else in Asia, and any business is expected to have wifi.

Will your hotel have free wifi? Your room is more likely to lack a bed than to lack free wifi. Free wifi is a basic requirement for a hotel in Vietnam. So is a bed, actually.

If you're in any shop or restaurant or other place of business in Vietnam, you can hand the staff your phone, with the wifi network selection screen opened, just say "wifi?" and they will very likely know they need to choose the network and enter the password for you. They do that dozens of times every day for all their customers. Usually the password will be 012345678 or 123456789. (There, I've just hacked Vietnam's entire WiFi infrastructure! Can I get a job at the NSA now? Srsly can I?)

Facebook is huge in Vietnam. Everything happens on Facebook, to a much greater degree than any other country I know of. Most businesses don't have a website, only a Facebook page, and don't have an email address, but do business through Facebook Messenger.

If there's some kind of hotel or other business in Vietnam you want to search for, you'd do well to search for it on Facebook. (Side note: It seems there are a few people claiming to be me on Facebook. None of them are me. I don't even use

Facebook. Ok, maybe I have a fake Facebook account I only use for spying on people. But I never told you that.)

College classes are taught through Facebook, and course syllabi are usually available only through Facebook. Most professors don't use email for talking with students but — you guessed it — Facebook Messenger. And so on.

The most popular messaging formats for Vietnamese people besides Facebook are Viber, Whatsapp (really only among the urban elite), WeChat (more popular in the North, closer to China), and Zalo and Zing (Vietnamese-only). Even if you are familiar with standard textbook Vietnamese, Vietnamese (just like any other language I guess) has a whole slew of terms of and abbreviations only used in online messaging. Get used to "khong" becoming "ko," "nhieu" becoming "nju," and a million others.

In addition to using the wifi that's available everywhere, you may want to use mobile data on your phone, especially for when you're on the street or on the road and not near wifi. 4G is absolutely everywhere in Saigon, and even 5G sometimes (in the neighborhoods where high-level Party members live).

As for mobile data service, in Vietnam, everyone uses prepaid SIM cards. I've never heard of anyone having a postpaid cellphone in Vietnam, unless it's on a corporate account. And we're generally not attached to our phone numbers. We might change SIM cards and providers and are more tied to our online IDs (especially Facebook and Zalo, WhatsApp among the more "urban and educated" set) and might not even have our phone numbers memorized. Maybe similarly to the way it is in your country, people under 30 or so almost never use voice phone calls, although older people need

MY SAIGON: THE LOCAL GUIDE TO HO CHI MINH CITY, VIETNAM

voice phone calls for everything and "don't trust the virtual world" (there's a Vietnamese expression for this).

So when we get SIM cards, it's all about the data. Our three main mobile phone carriers are Vinaphone, Mobifone, and Viettel, and they're always competing for the cheapest data plan. Right now the SIM card that I and my in-the-know friends use costs 150K VND ($6.30) for three months of unlimited data. That's not a typo. When three months are done, we dump the old SIM card and get a new one for another 150K VND. I'm telling you this not to brag, but to give you some idea of the going rates in-the-know Vietnamese people pay for SIM cards, and to tell you to watch out for airport and tourist-market vendors who want to charge you 500K VND for a SIM card with a small amount of data.

If you're planning on staying here long-term, you can start investigating the best cellphone plans and so on. I'm assuming you're coming for a few days or a few weeks, so a few dollars' price difference for your monthly internet doesn't really matter. On the other hand, from what I've seen of US cellphone carriers, data roaming in Vietnam on a US cellphone account is prohibitively expensive, so don't do that.

Here are your options for getting a SIM:

Get an e-SIM for Vietnam, if you have a phone that supports e-SIMs, before you set off on your trip. You can search Klook, eBay, and Google and there are tons of sellers of e-sims. That way, you won't have any physical SIM to worry about.

Or you can get a physical Vietnam SIM before you set off on your trip. Most online marketplaces such as eBay have them.

Another option is that before you travel, you can prepay for a Vietnam SIM that you'll pick up at the Saigon airport, from a site like Klook. You'll have the terms all set and a vendor to come back to should you have problems. I've heard good things about this service.

If you're a last-minute kind of person, you can buy a SIM from an airport vendor when you arrive. These are risky, and the SIMs they sell often don't have as much data as they claim and aren't valid for as long as they claim. There are many stories about them working for only a few hours or days. On the other hand, there are many stories about people being perfectly satisfied with their airport SIM purchases! You will of course pay a premium for buying from an airport vendor, but it might not be too bad: for example, at the airport you might pay 250,000 VND for a SIM that is available around Saigon for 100,000 VND. You could say that's 150% markup and it's outrageous, or you could say that's a difference of only six bucks for convenience and you won't sweat it.

If you have a Vietnamese friend, you can have them buy you a SIM on Lazada (the eBay-like site where we usually buy SIMs) and have it waiting for you at your hotel. You will need the Vietnamese friend because Lazada is only in Vietnamese and only accepts Vietnamese credit cards. Lazada does have the absolute best deals on SIMs, and it's where my friends and I get those 150K three-month SIMs.

Once you're in Saigon, you can go around small shops and street vendors and ask about a SIM. Yes, the random street vendors who sell drinks and snacks also sell SIM cards. The problem here is that getting a data plan is going to be a hassle, unless you find a shop that speaks English and knows data plans — somewhat rare.

MY SAIGON: THE LOCAL GUIDE TO HO CHI MINH CITY, VIETNAM

A better option once you're in Saigon is to go to either an official Vinaphone or Mobifone store (you can look for them on Google Maps) or a branch of our biggest cellphone shop, TheGioiDiDong (translates to Mobile World; there's one at 189A Cong Quynh right near the Pham Ngu Lao tourist area, and another one at 145 Nguyen Thi Minh Khai) and they will set you up. There are also two big offices of the big cellphone carriers, Vinaphone and Mobifone, right in central Saigon, both at 80 Nguyen Du (Monopoly isn't just a board game!) right in the center of the city. They'll speak decent English and they won't cheat you (famous last words?). The downside is you'll be wasting valuable vacation time doing phone setup. Remember to bring your passport if doing any phone stuff, or actually any stuff, at an official-type store. Street vendors don't care.

According to the law, anyone selling you a SIM card has to take your photo, and a photo of your national ID (for Vietnamese citizens) or your passport (for foreigners). The bigger the store, the more likely they'll actually follow this law. Bring your passport or something that looks like a passport when you go to buy your SIM card. You may want to specifically ask the seller about registration, because some SIM cards will stop working after a few days because there's no ID and photo on record for the user. Online and street vendors are generally immune from this law, and no, I don't know the details of why.

You can find out whether your sim card is registered by texting the letters TTTB followed by your passport number (so if your passport number is 12345, you'd send a message saying **TTTB 12345**) to the number 1414. If it's registered, it will reply with your name and other frighteningly detailed personal information. There is no way for you to register it yourself or to edit the information; this DIY method is only for viewing the info.

If you want to sign up for ride and delivery apps like Grab, Vinasun, and Gojek, make sure your SIM card 1) can accept incoming SMSs, as some SIMs don't and 2) hasn't been previously used to register for those services. A lot of cheap SIM cards, including those sold to tourists, are ones that were previously used by various bot farm operations to register for ride and delivery apps — and those SIM cards' phone numbers have been blacklisted from those apps. Some SIM cards sold on Lazada openly say that these are burner SIMs that have been used in bot farms and now can't be used to register for anything. What I suggest is you offer your SIM card seller a 20K VND or so tip (about $1) to help you register on Grab and any other apps when you buy your SIM.

Grab: the app you need

Grab is the app we use in Vietnam for rides, food delivery, convenience store delivery, and pretty much everything else.

You need this app, even if you're only in Saigon for a few days. You can use it for rides and food in all cities in Vietnam, and occasionally even in rural areas (if there are local drivers and businesses that have signed up with it).

I don't even like Grab. I've been to the US, and Uber and UberEats are a million times better than Grab. Grab has horrible customer service, a very clunky app, weird policies, and a lot of other problems. But there's no viable alternative here in Vietnam. Well, there are Be and Gojek, but they're even worse.

Unless you want to code your own app, or unless you want to get cheated by taxis, get Grab.

You can download the Grab app before you go to Vietnam, and can use a Google account or a Facebook account to log into it. It will also need to send you a verification message by SMS or WhatsApp, and as far as I know, that part will work fine even if your phone number is in the US (or another country that isn't Vietnam).

By default, payment for Grab services is in cash. You *can* pay by credit card, though. In the past, they didn't accept non-Vietnamese credit cards, but now they do. The only important thing: you have to be physically in Vietnam (or rather, your phone's GPS has to be reporting a location in Vietnam) in order to add a credit card to your Grab account.

I don't know why that is, but that's how it is, and it's not documented anywhere, and even Grab customer service reps don't know it. So either stick with using cash, or wait until you're in Vietnam to add the credit card.

Note that your US (or wherever you're from) bank may want to call you about the weird charge from a weird company called Grab, and your US phone isn't picking up (because you're in Vietnam), and your credit card might get fraud-blocked — I can totally imagine it happening. So be careful. Maybe if you're just on a short trip, stick with cash.

One of the best things about Grab is the food delivery option. You can have anything you want delivered pretty much any time day or night, with a delivery fee usually around 25,000 VND, about $1. (Thanks for the 5kg I gained during Covid; I couldn't have done it without you, GrabFood!) If you do have a credit card in Grab, it's a bit more convenient, because the delivery person can just drop off your food at your hotel and doesn't need to wait for payment. But if you're hungry, you'll be around waiting for your food anyway, right?

And always check the "offer codes" in the final order confirmation screen, as they always have discount codes available, but only if you find them and click on them. In my economics class I learned that this is called price discrimination!

Note that there's an option to use Grab to pay for things in physical stores and restaurants by scanning a QR code into your Grab app, but this is only available to Vietnamese citizens with Vietnamese bank accounts. And there are some other ancillary features of Grab (they apparently sell car insurance?!) that are only available to Vietnamese citizens. I don't think

MY SAIGON: THE LOCAL GUIDE TO HO CHI MINH CITY, VIETNAM

you're missing out on much by not having these features available to you as a non-citizen. (And if you are, lots of Vietnamese people would love to trade passports with you, mkay?)

You can use Grab in other Southeast Asian countries, such as Singapore, Indonesia, Malaysia, and Thailand. Just note that Grab will lock you out of your account if they see something "suspicious." Such as *Egads, yesterday you were in Vietnam, and today you're in Singapore; how is that humanly possible?! You must be a scammer!*.

Dealing with, or even contacting, Grab's "customer service" is a horrible, horrible experience (ask me how I know!). So be careful. If you're locked out of one Grab account, just use a different Google account and a new SIM to make a new Grab account. (Plz no Grab ban plz.)

Also: there's a new entrant to the Saigon ride app game, called Xanh SM or Xanh Taxi. Get the app from your preferred app store.

Xanh (it means *green*) is a division of Vinfast, the Vietnamese electric car company. I think this car service is going to be how they sell any of those Vinfast cars. Anyway, Xanh rides can be good, but you do need a Vietnamese phone number, it's often (but not always) more expensive than Grab, and sometimes there are no drivers available. The advantages though are that the cars are electric and both the cars and drivers tend to be nicer than those on Grab. You can pay with your credit card only inside the car (the driver has a credit card terminal), not in the app.

Shopping: the magic of grocery stores

I hate to be snarky. Well, no, maybe I thrive on it. But look. Foreigners always come to Vietnam wanting to shop at the traditional markets, the non-air-conditioned open-air places: the hotter and smellier the better.

The thing is, we Vietnamese people hate those places. We hated shopping in those places back when we had to, and were overjoyed when supermarkets came around. The "traditional markets" have poor quality, bad service, and high prices. That's the truth. Supermarkets have better stuff, lower prices, better service, and an all-around better experience. We're glad to have them.

Sure, get your Instagram pics at whatever stinky traditional market you want to go to. But I don't recommend you buy anything there. And keep an eye or better yet a hand on your wallet and your phone.

Especially for foods you want to bring home, like coffee and whatever else, but also souvenirs, t-shirts, and other random stuff, just go to a regular supermarket! I mean back in your home country, when you want to buy groceries, do you trudge around dirty, smelly wet markets, or do you just, you know, go to the supermarket? Vietnam is the same.

The absolute worst traditional market is Ben Thanh Market, what tourists usually call "the big market" or "the Saigon market." It's purely a tourist trap that will charge you higher prices than back in your country for made-in-China souvenirs the shop owners buy on Taobao. Really, stay away from that place. Saigonese people stopped going to Ben Thanh a long time ago, and stopped going to all "traditional" markets shortly thereafter.

So where do we Vietnamese people actually shop? The biggest buy-everything supermarket, the Walmart of Vietnam, is Lottemart. There's one in Q11 and another one in Q7. They're huge. They sell everything and even have food courts and movie theaters. In both cases, they're such huge landmarks that they *are* the addresses. There's no street address. Lottemart Q11 and Lottemart Q7 *are* the addresses. The one in Q7 is a bit bigger but the one in Q11 might be a bit closer to you.

There's also the Van Hanh Mall (11 Su Van Hanh, Q10), which is a mall that has a lot of supermarkets and supermarket-type stores, not like a US mall that's mostly clothing stores. And tons of other supermarkets around town: just do a Google or Grab search for *sieu thi*, the Vietnamese (and Cantonese) term for a supermarket.

Other than the Lottemarts and the Van Hanh Mall, two popular supermarket chains are Coopmart (there's one near Pham Ngu Lao at 189 Cong Quynh) and Vinmart (there's one at 72 Le Thanh Ton, near Ben Thanh Market).

Bye bye haggling, physically aggressive vendors, sketchy prices, pickpockets, puddles of pee, and all those other "traditional" experiences.

Vietnam's friendship ended with "traditional" markets. Supermarkets are our new best friend.

Tip-top tipping tips

Don't believe the guidebooks that say Vietnamese service staff will be insulted by tips, or that Vietnamese people never tip. Service staff love tips, and well-off Vietnamese people often tip.

I'm going to be very rude here, but I think most foreign travel writers in Vietnam are men who get their information about Vietnam from their Vietnamese girlfriends — girlfriends who tend to be from poor, rural backgrounds, and think that nobody in Vietnam tips.

A tip of 10K-20K (or a USD $1 bill) will be highly appreciated by everyone and will significantly raise their daily income. Tip your driver, your maid, your waiter, your front desk clerk, your tour guide, your street food vendor, even your cashier. (And cough cough, your policeman, although their tip expectation is usually in the 500K range.) Just don't tip with coins — those can't be used or exchanged in Vietnam.

No, tipping is not required, and anyone who tells you that a tip is mandatory is scamming you. Ben Thanh Market vendors tell foreign tourists that it's a "Vietnamese custom" to tip someone who sold you something. Uh, no. Although in Vietnam, it's not unheard of to tip a store employee who's been very helpful. Remember: service employees in Vietnam earn less than a dollar per hour, and are usually supporting multiple kids back in their villages.

The only place where tips should be a lot bigger than 10K-20K is massages. Generally for a massage, a minimum tip is 100K. That's because massage staff make negative salary.

They have to pay to work there, and they have to give the boss a cut of their tips too. Welcome to Workers' Paradise!

Wherever and whenever you tip in Vietnam, put the tip directly in the employee's hand if possible. Here in Workers' Paradise, bosses have very, very sticky fingers.

Relatedly, there's no concept of tipping based on the value of the bill. Don't think about percentages. Just think about raw amounts. Whether you're ordering 20K or 200K or 2,000K of food on GrabFood, a tip of 10K-20K is good, although of course the driver will be ecstatic if you give more.

Do Vietnamese people tip? Yes. Absolutely. At the upper echelons of society, people who can afford to tip are kind of expected to tip. It's still not universal, but it's very common to see your neighborhood bigshot put a 100K VND note under his finished bowl of pho. I once saw a neighborhood bigshot who has pho for breakfast at the same small restaurant every morning give the waitress 100 USD as a tip for Tet. It happens. Those are extremes, but 10K-20K-50K tips are common.

And tipping is the right way to "give back" or make a contribution to poor people in Vietnam or whatever you want to call it. As I say elsewhere in this book, any "nonprofits" or "charities" or "collection boxes" in Vietnam (yes, including the ones inside the airport and shopping malls) are scams. They're not scams to Some People who are raking in the cash. But they're scams for the tourists who think their money is going to a good cause. Unless you think some bigshot's new Bentley is a good cause.

Street safety and crime in Saigon

Are Saigon streets dangerous?
Compared with your sofa at home, yes, Saigon streets are dangerous!

Are Saigon streets more dangerous than those of other cities? No way!

Violent crime against strangers, especially foreign strangers, is unheard of in Saigon. Among my friends and family in Saigon, I don't know anyone who was the victim of *violent* crime.

A beatdown from your drunk cousin in a bar – well yes, that does happen in Saigon. Late-night gunfights between rival gangs in the outer districts tourists never visit – that also does happen. But unless you have drunk cousins or mafia enemies in Saigon, those risks shouldn't concern you.

The legal and social penalties for harming a foreigner are much harsher than those for harming a Vietnamese person. Colonial mindset? Maybe. But take advantage of it, and feel safe when you walk around Saigon.

Property theft, without any physical violence, is what happens most often in Saigon. Snatch and grab, almost always by two young guys on a motorcycle.

Almost every Saigonese person has had something stolen from them, usually in a drive-by motorcycle theft. Drive-by motorcycle thefts are pretty much equivalent to "Saigon crime." They're common, but they're as bad as it gets here. And the good news is that thanks to improved security on smartphones and things like "cloud lock," stealing phones has become less lucrative, and drive-by phone thefts are much less common now than they were a few years ago.

The risk of you encountering violent crime as a tourist in Saigon is pretty much zero. And to me, that's the important part. The gun holdups and "muggings" that we see in American movies are very rare in Saigon, to the point that I've never heard of it happening to anyone I know.

The not-so-good news is that small snatch-and-grab thefts, usually done by young guys on motorcycles, victimize all kinds of people. The thieves seem to have a supernatural sense of sight for spotting an expensive phone or handbag being held weakly in someone's hand near the road – and soon enough, that phone or handbag is gone. But if this happens, you don't lose your hand or your arm or your life. Only your phone or your handbag.

The other common thefts are more scams than thefts. There are two very common ones, both targeting horny foreign men.

In the most common Saigon scam for tourists, an attractive woman hits you up on a dating app or in a public place, and invites you to meet her at a specific place, often a specific bar. Of course she'll imply that there is boom-chika-chika-boom in store! If the bar she's working with has warnings about it already posted online, she'll ask to meet you at a public place nearby, then walk you over to the bar once you meet. Once you're in the bar, you'll have a nice time, you'll get drunk, and then she'll get an emergency phone call and have to go, while you'll get presented with a bill for a few thousand dollars. There will be gangsters blocking your exit.

MY SAIGON: THE LOCAL GUIDE TO HO CHI MINH CITY, VIETNAM

If you read this, you shouldn't let this happen to you. If it does, try to pay with your credit card, then immediately call your credit card company and dispute the charge. Or tell the gangsters you need to go to the ATM to get them their cash and then make a big public fuss once you're outside the bar. The police are likely in on this, so don't have too much faith in them, but the attention of a crowd of random strangers might be enough to get those gangsters away from you.

The second most common scam — this one usually run by Filipinos who are claiming to be Vietnamese — is someone striking up a conversation with you, then offering to set you up on a date with their supermodel niece. When you go to the place to meet the supermodel niece, she's not there, but there's an opportunity to "make some money by gambling" — and after a few hours, you owe somebody something like $10,000 USD, and you likely have ingested some sleeping drugs in the drinks they gave you. If this happens, again, try to get out of their reach and make a big scene in public. The police is less likely to work with these guys (because they're foreign), and if nothing else, strangers on the street will most likely help you out.

There is a strong mafia presence on all streets in central Saigon. These aren't movie gangsters who wear black suits. They look like just regular people on the street – who are usually involved as spotters for drive-by thefts, for coordinating beggars and trinket vendors, and for collecting "taxes" from business owners.

Nothing can happen on any street in central Saigon without mafia approval. Yes, that means that all the vendors and touts and beggars and "nice college students collecting money for charity" (cough cough) on the streets of central Saigon are either paying "taxes" to the mafia or are directly working for a mafia operation. I guess that's a subject for another book.

The Vietnamese term for mafia is *xa hoi den*, literally *black society*. Please don't make the American mistake of instantly thinking of races, because *black* here doesn't mean anything racial, but just means something illegal (like *black market*).

There are a few practical effects for you of the mafia presence in Saigon. One effect is that violent crime is very, very rare. Against tourists, even rarer. The mafia wants its streets to be safe and welcoming for business, for pedestrians, for tourists, and yes, for petty theft. They don't tolerate violent crime. Seriously, they don't. Young Dolph had love for the streets, and so does *xa hoi den*. Or love for money, at least.

The other thing is that reporting theft to the police will usually not yield any results for you. The police have deep connections with the mafia. Yes, the police will help you if you are in physical danger, but they won't care much if your phone was stolen (unless, perhaps, you offer to compensate them for their time and also to buy back the stolen item at a premium – which is indeed what Vietnamese people do when something like valuable data is stolen on an electronic device).

If something gets stolen from you, I do not advise wasting a day of your vacation reporting to the police, because they will give you the satisfaction of taking down a report and filling out forms, but you're unlikely to see your stuff returned. If it was valuable data stolen, you can try to ask your hotel to attempt to compensate the police and the thieves for getting the item back (generally you should expect to pay about the new retail price of the item), but I don't know if you want to spend your vacation time going through all that; it's better to leave your data in your hotel safe, or have it backed up to the cloud or to your mom's office computer (ok, this is what I used to do as a teenager).

If Saigon is safe from violent crime, why do many Saigonese people carry scars on their bodies? It's not from gun or knife fights, for sure. We're not Tupac. The biggest physical danger in Saigon is, by far, traffic accidents, and most people who have scars acquired them from being on a motorcycle in a traffic accident. Because of low speeds and mandatory helmets, deaths and life-threatening injuries are uncommon, but bruises and broken bones are very common.

Don't overlook traffic safety when considering your safety in Saigon. You're unlikely to face bodily harm from criminals, but you are much more likely to face bodily harm from falling off of a motorcycle taxi or a cyclo. It's strange how many tourists fret about "dangerous" Saigon but then happily hop on a cyclo (three wheels of death!) or on a motorcycle (two wheels of... broken arms and legs!).

We talked about Grab. Yes, Grab has Grab Bike, the motorcycle service. Yes, many Vietnamese people use it. I strongly, strongly recommend you don't get on any motorcycles in Vietnam, unless you just want to take a quick ride as a novelty. It's dangerous, very dangerous.

And if you think your Grab driver or the Grab company is going to help you if you get into an accident, you're living back in the first world. They won't help you. You'll be left to fend for yourself. You really don't want to have broken bones, or worse, on your vacation, just because you wanted to save fifty cents on a ride around town. Grab Car is not that much more expensive than Grab Bike. Use Grab Car, please, pretty please, with *nuoc mam* (fermented fish sauce) on top. I told you I'm a stick in the mud.

Sorry to be a fun spoiler, but the helmets used in Vietnam aren't good, car and especially truck drivers don't care about running over a mere motorcycle, there isn't a functional system of personal injury lawsuits like back in your country, and Vietnamese hospitals will not treat you without prepayment in cash. Staying off of motorcycles is my strong suggestion. Grab Car anywhere around the city should cost you well under 5 USD, usually more like 2 USD. That's well worth your safety.

The other big danger around Saigon? Look under your feet when you're walking around. Sidewalks can contain, in addition to speeding motorcycles: huge potholes, open sewers, open fires, full-scale open welding operations, dangerous chemicals, and pretty much everything else you can think of, all underfoot with no warnings given and no safety rules followed. One of the most common dangers in the tourist areas is street vendors who grill on the street and have handles and parts of their grill sticking out into the sidewalk — any tourist walking by might trip over the hot grill and come away with some very nasty burns. No, there are no personal injury lawyers in Vietnam. (We have *xa hoi den* though.)

Women's safety

The bad news is that sexual harassment and sexual assault are fairly common and fairly tolerated in Vietnam. Men openly leer at or make sexual remarks at middle-school girls, and nobody stops them (unless, of course, those girls are related to Some People, but that's another story). For most Vietnamese women, walking around Saigon includes having rude sexual remarks yelled at us, and sometimes seeing a delivery driver's wee-wee waved at us. It happens. And a taxi driver or a policeman might openly proposition us. That happens.

As for the really, really serious stuff? Yes, rape and blatant physical sexual assault do happen, but they're usually behind closed doors, and the perpetrators are known by the victims (boyfriends/husbands, relatives, teachers, or bosses). Date rape isn't even considered rape, and so on. However, physical sexual assault on Saigon streets *against strangers* in daylight is almost unheard of. Hooray, I guess?

And here's the most important part for you, as a woman: for whatever reason, the men who will leer and yell rape threats at a Vietnamese woman will be terrified to do so to a foreign (especially white) woman. That's for a number of reasons (including the language gap), but mostly because they believe foreign women won't put up with it, and will either bite the guy's balls off or report him somewhere or something. That also means, of course, that they believe that Vietnamese women *will* put up with it — and unfortunately to a large extent they're correct!

ELLY THUY NGUYEN

I would say if you're a white (or can be perceived as white) woman, then being leered at, and especially being physically touched, won't be a concern at all in Saigon, maybe unless you get into an environment of drunk men who aren't even thinking with their racism brains. If you're ethnically Vietnamese, or could be mistaken for such, these things are more of a threat, and I would generally recommend you avoid walking around at night, and especially (I really hate to say this, because it sounds like victim-blaming) avoid wearing revealing clothing on the street.

Sorry. That's Vietnam. Things are improving, but very, very slowly.

Covid precautions and masks

Masks are not required for tourists or visitors anywhere in Vietnam. There's no government mandate requiring wearing masks in any situation. I've never seen a business or office that requires customers to wear masks, although it's possible that one exists somewhere in Vietnam.

However, many service establishments such as restaurants and stores do require all their employees to wear masks. And many people in Vietnam wear masks as a habit — for the pollution and also for the sun — and we've been doing it even before Covid.

If you care about wearing high-quality N95 masks, bring them from your country. The masks sold here look nice, but any N95 markings on them are fake and meaningless.

In Vietnam there are none of the "culture wars" about masks and vaccines that you have in the US. Oh, we have lots of culture wars of our own (we had a big one fifty years ago; maybe you've heard of it?), but not about Covid stuff. Don't expect any weird looks regarding whether you wear a mask.

Hotels and business establishments still officially advertise, especially in foreign media and on foreign travel websites, that they have mandatory temperature checks and onsite doctors and social distancing and things like that, but none of that actually happens in reality.

There are no Covid-based entry requirements or restrictions in Vietnam. Covid antigen tests are widely available in pharmacies for about 100K VND a test.

ELLY THUY NGUYEN

For effective medical treatment for Covid or anything else, I recommend FV Hospital. Most other practitioners and pharmacies here rely on voodoo magic, oops, "traditional Vietnamese medicine." (Cough cough, which is actually traditional Chinese medicine, which is just a bunch of incongruent folk tales and superstitions.)

MY SAIGON: THE LOCAL GUIDE TO HO CHI MINH CITY, VIETNAM

Vietnamese language reference

People in the tourist industry in Vietnam speak English well. Speak English slowly and clearly, be ready to write things down with a pen or on your phone, and you should do ok. But that's only the tourist industry. If you want to go outside the tourist haunts – which is what this book is all about, after all – the English level is much lower.

Actually, people from Saigon, especially those who attended college, usually speak pretty good English. But people from Saigon who attended college usually work in offices, and are not the people you'll encounter working in a cafe or a taxi or other service establishment. The Grab drivers, cafe servers, fruit vendors, shoe cleaners, and other service-industry people you may encounter in Saigon are not from Saigon, but from Vietnam's much poorer rural areas. (It's like this: Is someone mowing lawns or cleaning toilets in Beverly Hills born and raised in Beverly Hills? Probably not. Saigon is the Beverly Hills of Vietnam.)

Stereotypically, all the service employees in Saigon come from a region called Mien Tay – which translates to Western Fields – the rural provinces immediately to the west of Saigon. Foreigners usually call that region "the Mekong delta," but in Vietnamese, it's called Mien Tay.

Of course, people come from all over Vietnam (and Cambodia, Laos, and the Philippines) to work in Saigon, but most service people you encounter will be from Mien Tay – and will have very little English, perhaps other than the few phrases they've been taught by their boss. Public schools charge high tuition fees here in our socialist paradise country, and most families can't afford much schooling for their kids. And English isn't really taught in rural schools.

There aren't many cognates between Vietnamese and English, so you can't hope to make yourself understood by speaking English slowly to people who simply don't know English. Knowing a few words of Vietnamese is really your only solution.

What are the advantages of knowing a little bit of Vietnamese language? You'll get a lot of smiles, and maybe even a lot of admiration, for taking a shot at speaking Vietnamese. And with just a little bit of up-front effort, you'll avoid a great deal of the frustration tourists face in Vietnam.

My quick Vietnamese language tutorial is a crash course, to make sure you don't crash when you're here. It's not anything more than that, so please don't criticize me for not teaching you the fine nuances of literary Vietnamese to prepare you for publishing your world-acclaimed book of classical Vietnamese poetry. That's not what this guide is for.

The first part of this guide is a list of sounds, very basic words (including numbers), and concepts. If possible, you should memorize everything in the first part. The second part is a list of some more words that may be useful for you, and you can look up as you need, especially when reading signs or menus. I won't stop you if you try to memorize the second part too, but I think it might be too much commitment if you're just a tourist coming to Saigon!

As far as a casual tourist is concerned, written Vietnamese is pronounced closely to what you would expect from the Roman alphabet. You can sound out the words even if you're not an expert in Vietnamese. No, you won't sound like a native speaker if you follow this method. But that's not what this guide is about.

The big differences between English and Vietnamese pronunciation of letters are a few consonant sounds. D without a horizontal line through it is pronounced like *y* in "yankee." GI is also pronounced like *y* in "yankee." So the popular Vietnamese female name *Dung* is pronounced *Yoong* (so stop laughing at how you think it might be pronounced), and fried spring rolls, *cha gio*, is pronounced *cha yo*. In Hanoi, those would be pronounced *Zoong* and *cha zo*.

"Nh" if beginning a word is pronounced like the n in "new" or in the children's taunt "nyah nyah nyah!" So, for example, the word for "restaurant" is "nha hang," pronounced "nya hang." And a popular name for a man is Nhan, pronounced "Nyan." "Nh" at the end of the word, as in Ben Thanh Market, is pronounced like a regular "n."

"Ch" at the beginning of the word is pronounced as in Charlie. At the end of the word, it's pronounced as T. So the popular female name *Bich* is pronounced *Bit*. Not the way some of you misogynists might hope it's pronounced.

"Tr" is, strictly speaking, pronounced like the "tr" in "tree," but in daily speech, it's more like "ch" in "choice" or "cherry." So if you want to order iced tea, it's "tra da," pronounced "cha da."

Remember those marks on vowels, called diacritics? The ones that I won't include in this book? Those do make some difference in pronunciation. But there's no simple way for a beginner to learn how they work – you would have to put a few good weeks into learning diacritics, so we won't bother with that here. But if a word, especially a vowel, turns out to be pronounced differently from how you expected, it's probably the diacritics at work.

Let's start with the numbers. You'll need this for prices. I recommend that you memorize the words for numbers 1-10, and the words for hundred and thousand – and you will be ahead of 99.9% of the tourists in Saigon. I've casually talked with some market sellers at Ben Thanh market in Saigon, and they said they have *never* seen a tourist who could say the numbers in Vietnamese.

MY SAIGON: THE LOCAL GUIDE TO HO CHI MINH CITY, VIETNAM

0 le / khong
1 mot
2 hai
3 ba
4 bon / tu (*boon / too*)
5 nam (*nam* or sometimes *lam* if last digit)
6 sau
7 bay
8 tam (*taaaam* to differentiate from *nam*)
9 chin
10 muoi
100 tram (*cham*)
1000 ngan / nghin (*nyan* in Saigon, *nin* in Hanoi)
10,000 muoi ngan
100,000 mot tram ngan
1,000,000 mot trieu (*chieu*)

Numbers above 10 are formed by using what you already know. For example, 11 is muoi mot (ten one). 111 is tram muoi mot (hundred ten one).

Zero is formally *khong*, but in Saigon, usually *le*. (*Khong* is the same word as "no" or "nothing." The Saigonese *le* is just a shortening of *ling*, the Chinese word for zero.)

You may sometimes encounter *tu* instead of *bon* in formal contexts, but in daily life, we use *bon*, which is sort of a euphemism for *tu*. That has to do with the Sinitic tradition of avoiding direct reference to the number four in reference to people and the Sinitic cultural associations of the number four with death. The anthropological term for this tradition is *tetraphobia*. Look it up.

ELLY THUY NGUYEN

You'll need to use zero (*le*) in Vietnamese more often than you'd need it in English. Suppose you want to convey the number 102. If you say "tram hai" (hundred two) in Vietnamese, a Vietnamese speaker understands it as 120, not 102. So it's better to say "tram le hai" (hundred zero two) or "mot le hai" (one zero two) to make it clear you mean 102, not 120.

Thanks to the huge inflation in Vietnam in the 1980s, you won't see money below 1,000 dong (which is about $0.04 USD). Get used to saying and hearing *nyan* (thousand) a lot. And sometimes in colloquial speech, people drop the word for thousand. So if a street vendor tells you a baguette costs "hai muoi," (twenty) you can be pretty certain that's twenty thousand dong ($0.80), not twenty dong ($0.0008)!

Advanced lesson, for advanced students, and extra credit: in Vietnamese slang, 10,000 dong is "chuc" (*chook*), 100,000 dong is "xi" (*see*), and 1,000,000 dong is "chai" or "chanh." Vendors would not be so slangy with a foreigner, but if selling something to a Vietnamese person, they would very often talk about *chuc*, and sometimes about *xi* or *chai*. For example, they might quote the price of something as "bay chuc" (*bay chook*) – this means seven times 10,000 dong, so 70,000 dong. If you want to shock someone with your intimate knowledge of Saigon slang, feel free to talk about "chuc" and "xi" and "chai" and "chanh"! It's like saying "bucks" in American English or "quid" in British English.

These slang terms for money started as codewords that gambling bookies used when they didn't want to make it obvious they were talking about money. (Bookies! We're a city of bookies. I don't know of any city other than Saigon where

MY SAIGON: THE LOCAL GUIDE TO HO CHI MINH CITY, VIETNAM

bookies wander the neighborhood streets, proactively asking people to bet on something, anything, but usually soccer matches.)

In addition to numbers, here are basic words everyone should know. I won't worry about spelling them for you. I'll just tell you how to pronounce them.

Yes - Ya
No - Khong
Thank you - Kahm ung
How much (money)? - Bao nyoo (teen)?
Sorry / excuse me - Sin loi
Check or bill - Tan tien
Correct / true - Phai
Wrong / false - Khong phai
Can you do it? / Is it possible? - Dook khong?
Possible / can be done - Dook
Impossible / can't be done - Khong dook
Alright / ok – Yoy
Right (direction) - Phai
Left (direction) - Chai
Bathroom - Ve seen
Where is X? - X o dau?
Here - O day
Over there - O do
Stop here (slangy, for taxi) - Yu day
Eat a meal - An com
Drink (water / tea / beer / liquor) - Uong (nook soi / cha / bia / rou)
Restaurant - Nya hang
Water - Nook soi

I know these words sound like alien talk to you. They're so different from English that you don't have anything to refer to. You just have to get used to the sounds. My suggestion is that you try practicing these words many times before your trip, at first reading them from this book, then maybe saving them on your phone or a piece of paper.

When you've heard yourself saying these words a hundred times, they will start to stay in your head – and they won't sound like alien talk anymore. At least Vietnamese, unlike most Asian languages, is written using the Roman alphabet, so you will start to recognize some of the things written on signs and in public places.

And on that note, here are some translations of signs you might commonly see around Saigon:

Bang gia - price list
Cac loai - all types
Cam - prohibited
Can tuyen - help wanted (we're hiring)
Canh sat – police
Cap cuu - emergency
Chuyen - service/serving/offer
Dac biet - specialty
Duong - street or road
Du lich – tourist
Giam gia - discount
Giu xe - parking
Hem - alley
Hot toc - barbershop
Khach san - hotel
Mien phi - free

MY SAIGON: THE LOCAL GUIDE TO HO CHI MINH CITY, VIETNAM

Mo cua - hours of operation
Nam - men
Nguoi lon - adults
Nu / phu nu - women
Nha hang - restaurant
Phong kham - medical clinic
Quy khach - dear customer
Rua xe - car and motorcycle wash
Tiem an - small restaurant
Tre em - children
Uon toc - beauty salon
Xoa bop - massage

And, just for fun, some very Saigonese slang for you, that you might be able to use to shock, impress, and amuse your waiters, bellmen, or new Vietnamese friends:

bo tay - "my hands are tied," mock frustration at a situation
cay si - "tree root," hopeless romantic who won't give up
con de (*con ye*) - "goat," lecher or pervert
cuoc song ma - "that's life," used like "oh well!"
di cho - "go to the market," choose from a menu
di choi - "go enjoy," go out to have fun
keo ly - "glue," someone who has a longtime crush on you
mo nhon (*mo nyon*) - "sharp beak," a smooth talker
nha que – rural or provincial person or place, a "hick"
so mot - "number one," the best at something
soai ca - a very handsome man
taxi du (*taxi yu*) - "parachuting taxi," a dishonest taxi
tay ba lo - "Western backpack," a backpacker
trai bao - "payment boy," a gigolo
troi dat oi - "god earth oh," expressing shock or frustration

tum bay tum ba - "grab seven, grab three," talking nonsense

For non-slang Vietnamese, you can look on any website or Google Translate, but I'm giving you this Saigon slang because you can't easily find it in reference books.

There is one topic of standard Vietnamese, however, that I'd like to explain to you, because it's so central to Vietnamese language and even Vietnamese culture: that in Vietnamese, we almost always refer to people in the third person in daily speech.

There's no "I" or "you" in Vietnamese. Well, almost not. We do have some words that are used as "I" and "you," but they are almost never used in South Vietnam. The formal Vietnamese words for "I" and "you" are like saying "thou" or "thine" in English; they are real words, but no one uses them in Saigon (they are used in Hanoi though), and you would look ridiculous trying to use them in daily life.

In Vietnamese, everyone is generally addressed only with the third person. No I. No you. Only third person. (This becomes less true the farther north you go in Vietnam, but this is a Saigon book.)

There is a complex system of third-person pronouns in Vietnamese, all based on family relationships. For example, you call a man who is about your age or slightly older "anh," which means "older brother." And when I say "call a man," that includes yourself if you're a man.

If you are talking with someone who you think should regard you as an older brother, you call yourself "anh" instead of saying "I," and you call the other person "em," which is a younger sibling. *Anh* and *em* are by far the most commonly

MY SAIGON: THE LOCAL GUIDE TO HO CHI MINH CITY, VIETNAM

used pronouns. In daily life you pretty much call everyone, other than very old or very young people, *anh* and *em*.

Yes, it sounds funny if directly translated to English. While an English speaker might say "I'm happy to see you," a Vietnamese speaker might say something that directly translates as *Older brother is happy to see younger sibling*. It sounds really awkward in English, but it sounds natural in Vietnamese – partly because the words for *older brother* and *younger sibling* are short one-syllable words (*anh* and *em)* very commonly heard in daily conversation.

For extra credit: *anh* is often abbreviated to *A* and *em* is often abbreviated to *E*. Hence the name of the Vietnamese hotel chain *A&Em* really means *Anh & Em*. (*A&Em* are pretty reliable midrange hotels around Saigon, by the way. Consider them the Holiday Inn of Saigon.)

The whole system of the proper third-person words to use to address someone is a big topic. And even Vietnamese people often disagree on the proper way to address someone. But here's the important thing: once you have learned these terms, you've pretty much mastered a big portion of the politeness and respect in Vietnamese culture!

So the terms of familial relationships are indeed a big topic, but because they are such a big thing, they pretty much cover and encapsulate all types of politeness. If there were a Miss Manners in Vietnam (and we do have them, usually nosy aunties), much of what she would concern herself with is what terms of address you should use for various people. And you can even see this in Vietnamese popular culture: "What words should we use to call each other?" is a very common topic in any movie or novel or even song about friendships, relationships, or families. It's similar to the line "What am I to you?"

Insert joke about American culture wars and "pronouns." Or don't. We have enough culture wars (and in the past, actual wars) in Vietnam.

Now that I've convinced you that there's no commonly used "you," is that really true even in the most direct situations? Is it true even if you're just yelling to someone on the street? Yes, it's true.

To get someone's attention on the street, you would say their title (such as *anh* or *em*) followed by *oi*, which sounds just as it's spelled. *Oi* is the Vietnamese version of *hey!* For example, *anh oi!* (hey, older brother!) or *chi oi!* (hey, older sister!) or *em oi*! (hey, younger sibling!) – you might hear those around Saigon, especially when someone calls a waiter or waitress in a restaurant.

But I told you that there *are* direct words for I and you, so what are they? In case you are wondering what those words are – here is a summary.

The most common (still uncommon, but relatively common) way to say I as the speaker is *toi*. In Saigon, you would almost exclusively encounter it in written Vietnamese, in very formal situations, or in something like a website or an announcement, and very rarely in daily speech. (Although as I mentioned, it's somewhat common in Hanoi and northern areas.)

Again, it's like saying *thou* in the US in the Year of Our Lord 2024. Every guidebook and phrasebook teaches you to say *toi*, and people will understand you if you say *toi*, but it sounds weird.

MY SAIGON: THE LOCAL GUIDE TO HO CHI MINH CITY, VIETNAM

There is also its less formal Saigonese derivative, *tui*. *Tui* is actually used sometimes in Saigonese speech, but not often, and it's considered "not a real word" by language powers that be.

The most common way to say *you* in daily life when you're uncertain of the other person's gender and status (for example, online) is *ban*, pronounced *baahn*. Literally it means *friend*. Using it for *you* is a new usage that came mostly with technology and commercialization in Vietnam. In the old days, you always saw someone (and usually even knew someone) if you were speaking to them, so you could choose the right way to address them. But if you are writing a webpage and want to address your audience, or writing to a customer service representative, you have no idea of the other person's gender, age, and status, nor even whether you're talking to one person or many – so around the early 2000s we Vietnamese people started using *ban* as this form of *you*.

Note that *ban* means *friend*, but you would never address your friend as ban. Actually English is similar. It would be very strange in English if you addressed your friend as *friend*.

Many Vietnamese language learning guides tell you that you should use *toi* to say I and *ban* to say you. That is somewhat correct, in that Vietnamese people will definitely understand what you mean, but no native speaker would ever say it that way. You will sound like a train station announcement or a propaganda poster. We usually say *anh* and *em* and *chi*. The only time we might say *toi* is when in a conversation it becomes confusing who is (for example) *anh* and who is *em* and then we might switch to *toi* (or *tui*) and *ban* to make it clear.

The other two terms for *I* and *you*, I'm not sure whether I should tell you. But for completeness I will. They are *tao* for *I* and *may* for *you*. *They are very rude and aggressive and will get you beaten up or worse!*

Calling yourself *tao* and the other person *may* is like using profanity.

Remember how I said that using the proper terms of address is the big part of politeness in Vietnamese language? Well, using *tao* and *may* is all it takes to make what you're saying sound very rude! In most contexts it is not only rude but aggressively incendiary. It's what drunk guys start saying to one another when they're trying to start a fight.

Some young people and very close friends do call one another *tao* and *may* in good fun, but it requires very close friendship (and maybe a good sense of humor) to be able to use those words without insult. I guess in English it's the same. In English, friends might have terms of address for each other that sound offensive. In Vietnamese those are *tao* and *may*. Never use them, unless you are really sure of what you're doing. And I hope you never hear them either.

As a funny side note, in the pre-1975 days, and especially in the French colonial days, the French language was fashionable in Saigon. Most Saigonese people wanted to speak French, but not many actually knew French.

So, to be fashionable, many Vietnamese people used the French *moi* and *toi* in their Vietnamese speech, solving two problems at once: the lack of *I* and *you* in Vietnamese, and their need to appear fashionable!

No one uses *moi* and *toi* anymore in daily speech, unless they're old people reminiscing about the old days. But nowadays young Vietnamese people do sometimes say *I* and *you* in English while speaking Vietnamese, for very similar reasons.

"You you you!"

Your first day in Saigon, when you walk out on the street, the first thing that you might hear said to you (or yelled at you) is *you you you you you you!* Why? What's going on?

It relates to the previous section, where I explained to you that the Vietnamese language doesn't have "I" and "you." Almost all of the street vendors and other people hanging around Q1 serving tourists are from poor, rural, low-education backgrounds. Back in their villages, they might have had very little formal schooling (by the way, school, even elementary school, isn't free in Vietnam), or no schooling at all.

What does their education have to do with it? Well, it's what they've been told about the English language. They've been told the most amazing thing about the English language: that while in Vietnamese, there are dozens of forms of second-person address, and you might call someone twenty different words in twenty different contexts, in English, there is only one word, "you."

This is a wonderment to a Vietnamese person. Instead of all the complexities of Vietnamese pronouns, English only has the word "you."

Of course, you and I know that English is not so simple. But that is "English 101" that someone in a remote village might have received before they set off to their job in Saigon.

So, as far as they're concerned, the magic word in English is "you." And in order to say the equivalent of "Dear chap, might I trouble you to buy these sunglasses I'm selling?" all they have to say is "you." And to convey urgency and emphasize the good deal on the sunglasses, they just have to yell "you" loudly, and repeat it many times. Any time street vendors or other non-English-fluent people want to get your attention, they'll likely start yelling and repeating "you you you!"

Yes, we Vietnamese people who studied English know how silly "you you you" sounds. When we joke to one another about badly spoken English, we say "you you you!" because we know that's what is often said to tourists.

But word is getting out, because in some of the most heavily trafficked tourist places, such as Ben Thanh Market, vendors are now saying "Sir! Madam!" or other more appropriate equivalents, instead of just yelling "you you you!" It does mess with their worldview a bit, because previously, a cornerstone of their beliefs about English was that any person-to-person contact could be contained in a yelled "you you you!"

The other thing that street vendors have learned to yell, sometimes when you're walking past them, is "WAIT! WAIT!" They know that this gets an English speaker's attention. You might have to spend a few hours or days training yourself to change your instincts and not stop dead in your tracks when you hear someone yell "WAIT!" (See, the vendors are very smart that way.)

"Motorbike!"

The next thing you'll probably hear after hearing "you you you" is "motorbike!" That is someone offering you their services as a motorcycle chauffeur. The Vietnamese term for that is "xe om." "Xe" is a vehicle, and "om" means hugging—so it's a hugging vehicle, because the passenger has to hug the driver to hold on.

The people offering this service are not full-time professional motorcycle chauffeurs. They're just guys who, upon seeing a foreigner, want to make some extra cash and offer them a ride. These guys used to be the most common form of transport around Saigon, but now they're pretty much extinct, replaced not only by personal vehicle ownership, but also by Grab.

Many of these drivers are unable to to be hired by the app-based services because they're too old (yes, all kinds of discrimination are legal, blatant, and pervasive in Vietnam) or because they were fired for misconduct or they have a criminal record. They often will be wearing a Grab uniform, but those uniforms can be bought at any corner store in Vietnam, and no matter what those guys say, they have no affiliation with Grab.

Going with these guys is a really bad idea. They will rip you off. They know that tourists don't know distances and prices, so you can expect to pay more than for a regular taxi. We Vietnamese people almost never go with these guys (exception: sometimes someone will establish a long-term relationship with such a guy to drive them on a daily commute at a preset time and place and price, and that's more convenient than having to click an app every day), so why should you?

What's worse, you can be almost certain that there will be sales pitches for souvenirs, prostitutes, hotels, drugs, and whatever else pays a commission, and there might even be unscheduled stops at places selling those.

And even worse, they're not particularly safe drivers, and if you crash, they're certainly not going to cover your medical bills, nor even stick around to call an ambulance. They are notorious for disappearing after an accident.

Be careful. If you want to ride on a motorcycle (which I don't particularly recommend), get the Grab app. It's not perfectly safe, but it's better than riding with those... moto-randos. (Hey, that's pretty good.)

You called me what?

In first-world countries, it's rude to refer to people by their races. I know. But in Vietnam, it's normal. I'm sorry, but that's how it is.

If you're white (and no, I don't know exactly what the average Vietnamese person considers white or non-white), your name in Vietnam is "Tay." It means West. It applies to men, women, children, anyone. It's used as both a noun and an adjective. And if you're white and you walk into some of the places I recommend that don't see many non-Vietnamese customers, you might hear the word "Tay!" announced loudly, or whispered conspiratorially.

You're not expected to know that "Tay" is your name. But now you know. And now you might know when people are talking about you. And no, even if you and your family have lived in Europe or North America for ten generations, if your ethnic background isn't white, you'll never be called Tay.

If you're not white, but clearly aren't from around here, you present something of a problem to the patented Vietnamese ultra-quick racial categorization system. You will likely fall into two mental categories: "Viet kieu" (pronounced *yiet kyoo*) or "nuoc ngoai" (pronounced *nook noai*). A Viet kieu is an ethnically Vietnamese person who lives permanently outside Vietnam. Nuoc ngoai is a general "and all others" kind of term for foreigner, literally meaning "from outside."

If your appearance suggests an East Asian ethnic background, it's likely you'll be assumed to be Viet kieu. Congratulations. You are now very rich, very foolish, speak

Vietnamese incorrectly (or not at all), and come to Vietnam to look down on Vietnamese people. Saigon street vendors don't take much pleasure in overcharging "Tay" (white people), but there's a lot of sly pleasure in overcharging and generally cheating and berating "Viet kieu."

Nuoc ngoai, pronounced *nook noay*, is a catch-all term meaning "foreigner." If you are not white and not ethnically Vietnamese, you will likely be called nuoc ngoai.

What's the purpose of teaching you these terms? It's just so you know when people are talking about you. Just because you're paranoid doesn't mean they're not talking about you. Or something like that.

The Saigon no

Sometimes, no matter how attractive the offer of conical rice paddy hats and sunglasses and coconuts from the lovely street vendor, you have to say no.

Guidebooks tell you to say *khong*, which is a literal translation of *no*. In practice, saying *khong* makes you sound like a tourist who is parroting a guidebook (not this one, of course).

There's a better way to convey *no*. One magic Saigonese hand gesture can ward off street sellers, beggars, and anyone else you don't want to deal with. It can also be useful when your friends accuse you of a misdeed you deny. It's how fishermen show they didn't catch anything, taxi drivers show they can't take a passenger, and soup vendors show they're all out of broth. This silent hand gesture is the closest thing in Vietnamese to a definite "no."

It goes like this: hold your right arm up, with the palm relaxed, and "twist" your hand as if you're quickly unscrewing a lightbulb. Some people call it a "sped-up Queen of England wave." The Queen of England has never waved to me, so I can't be sure. But I do know it resembles the motion of turning a lightbulb.

The Saigonese *no* gesture is most often used in commerce, such as when indicating you don't want to buy something or don't want a salesperson to bother you, or telling a waiter you don't need a refill of tea. It can also be used in social conversation, instead of or in addition to verbal negatives, when you want to vehemently deny something.

Where to stay?

There are hotels on every corner in Saigon. It's a very, very competitive market. Unless you just love to spend money, don't stay in one of the big chain hotels like Hyatt or Sofitel or Sheraton, because the prices are five to ten times the price of a perfectly good room at a smaller hotel.

The Hyatt/Sofitel/Sheraton hotels cost around $300 USD per night. Yes, it's a ripoff, considering prices and salaries in Vietnam. $300 is a blue-collar monthly salary in Saigon. But business in Vietnam is booming, and they know that most big foreign companies are not comfortable putting up their employees in small, locally owned hotels. But you, on the other hand, are comfortable putting yourself up in a small, locally owned hotel, right? Especially for 1/10th the price of those big places.... right?

Many tourists like to stay in Pham Ngu Lao, which is the backpacker district. Yes, it has many competitive hotels. And yes, most everything in Pham Ngu Lao is in English.

I hate Pham Ngu Lao though. It's a nasty, dirty cesspool, and it really has nothing to do with the real Saigon.

Specifically, I have four reasons I recommend against you staying in Pham Ngu Lao: 1) It's really nothing Vietnamese; 99% of the people you see in Pham Ngu Lao are either foreign tourists or people working in the tourist industry, 2) It is loud and rowdy at night, 3) A lot of pickpockets and drug dealers and other objectionable people (both Vietnamese and foreign) hang out there, 4) Even the "nicer" hotels in Pham Ngu Lao resemble hostels.

Well, if your idea of fun is getting drunk with foreign backpackers, stepping over puddles of vomit, and hanging out with drug dealers, pickpockets, and prostitutes, maybe you'll enjoy Pham Ngu Lao. I don't. (Vietnamese slang lesson: *tay ba lo*, Western backpack. Previously it was an insult for something like low-class tourists who were looked down upon, but now it's becoming a neutral term for all backpackers in Vietnam. I was shocked the first time I saw an official Saigon tourist map that labeled Pham Ngu Lao as *Tay Ba Lo District*.)

Instead of Pham Ngu Lao, I recommend that you stay near Ben Thanh Market, especially around Ly Tu Trong and Le Thanh Ton streets. It's walking distance to Pham Ngu Lao and to all of touristy Saigon, and it still has a good proportion of English language speaking and tourist "stuff," but it doesn't have Pham Ngu Lao's bad traits.

The most important street for hotels in the neighborhood I recommend is Ly Tu Trong street. Ly Tu Trong is a street running directly from Ben Thanh Market, and almost every establishment on the street is a hotel.

There are so many great hotel options on Ly Tu Trong and so much competition that it wouldn't be honest if I recommended you just one hotel or even a list of a few hotels on this street. There are dozens, and as far as I know, none is bad. (In fact, if anyone recommends just one hotel on this street, you can be sure they have a financial interest in it! All small hotels pay commissions to people who bring them guests.)

If you absolutely want a recommendation: try any of the A & Em hotels on Ly Tu Trong or Le Thanh Ton streets (see a-emhotels.com). They are a small chain and known to be

MY SAIGON: THE LOCAL GUIDE TO HO CHI MINH CITY, VIETNAM

reliable, and the A & Em at 280 Le Thanh Ton (on the corner of Le Thanh Ton and Le Anh Xuan) is a particularly nice location. Confession: when I have relatives visiting, I always recommend that A & Em hotel to them. I think it's a good choice. But it's only one choice out of many, and you don't have to do what I do.

Remember the lesson on Vietnamese pronouns? The name A & Em refers to the most common Vietnamese pronouns, Anh and Em. Anh is often abbreviated just to the letter A. So the hotel name means something like "You and I."

Most any hotel on Ly Tu Trong or Le Thanh Ton will most likely be great. It's such a competitive market and the hotels are so similar that it really would not be fair, nor useful, for me to point you to one hotel over another. Of course, you can take a look on Tripadvisor and similar websites, but small hotels in Vietnam are notorious for fake online reviews.

For actually booking the hotel, there's an Asian hotel booking site you may not be familiar with: Agoda. The good thing about Agoda is that for hotels in Vietnam, its prices are often much cheaper than the prices on Expedia or even directly through the hotel. I am talking like half the Expedia price. The bad thing about Agoda is its customer service and general customer experience are terrible. Agoda is a very frustrating company to deal with, and their customer service is nonexistent (I've got stories!), but their low prices might make up for it. You get what you pay for, I guess.

I suggest that before you arrive, you book one or two nights online in any hotel you like on Ly Tu Trong or Le Thanh Ton, and once you've arrived, take a look around at other hotels, ask them for their best price offers, and see whether you want to stay in your original hotel, or move on to a new place.

When you've finally decided on a hotel, compare their Agoda price to the price quoted by the front desk. Often Agoda is cheaper.

When you're asking about room rates in Vietnam, remember that Vietnam, probably unlike your country, doesn't have strong safety and sanitation requirements for hotel rooms. What this means is that cheaper hotel rooms are often windowless, and might not even get any fresh air. They feel like a closet. So be careful that you check the room that you're being quoted a price on. Usually the windowless rooms are called the "basic" or "standard" rooms, and the more palatable (to your tastes) rooms, with windows, might be called "superior" or "luxury" or "deluxe" or something like that, and cost a few dollars more per night. Although some hotels do call their windowless rooms "superior" or "deluxe," so be careful.

Every hotel in Vietnam (other than maybe the very expensive five-star hotels) provides free wifi to its guests. Every hotel provides free toiletries, toothbrushes, and toothpaste, although that hotel toothpaste might taste like... hotel toothpaste! You can easily buy toiletries at a Circle K store, the convenience stores that are everywhere.

Yes, there's hot water in Vietnam. Yes, the toilets flush. Yes, foreigners do ask these questions about Vietnam.

As for whether the tap water is drinkable? The official Vietnamese government line is that yes, it's drinkable. Any Vietnamese person will tell you that you'll instantly drop dead if you swallow a drop of Vietnamese tap water. I think the truth is in the middle. I think the water that comes out of the Saigon

MY SAIGON: THE LOCAL GUIDE TO HO CHI MINH CITY, VIETNAM

water plant is drinkable, but there are many dirty, corroded, and otherwise unsanitary pipes downstream, especially inside old buildings. So I would recommend you avoid drinking the tap water unless it's an emergency. Yes, it's fine for brushing your teeth and rinsing your mouth.

Do you know the famous photo taken in April 1975, of South Vietnamese people rushing to get on a US military helicopter on a building rooftop, in order to be evacuated out of Vietnam as Saigon fell? That photo was taken at 22 Ly Tu Trong Street (of course, the street had a different name at that time; Ly Tu Trong is the post-1975 name).

The building is still there. There's a myth that those people getting on the helicopter were US soldiers. No, they were Vietnamese people, most of them employees of the US government in Saigon.

What does *Ly Tu Trong* mean anyway? Ly Tu Trong is the name of a boy who set himself on fire to blow up a South Vietnamese military fueling station, for the glory of North Vietnamese dictatorship and destroying the evils of South Vietnamese democracy. Schoolchildren in Vietnam are taught about Ly Tu Trong's heroism.

Here's a little secret though. Don't feel too bad for the underage suicide bomber, because, um, he never existed. It's just a made-up propaganda story to make kids respect and emulate, I don't know, child terrorists? Shh. You didn't hear it from me. There are quite a few Saigon streets named after Communist heroes whose historical existence is, uh, debatable. But you didn't hear it from me.

Dollars and dong

Nowadays, everyone in Saigon uses Vietnamese dong for pretty much everything. In fact, Vietnamese law stipulates that all transactions within Vietnam must be done in Vietnamese dong. People still use US dollars to buy things like cars and houses (yes, despite that law), but for anything in your everyday life it's going to be Vietnamese dong.

If a vendor or an establishment quotes you a price in US dollars, it's a sign that the item is overpriced. There's no logical reason for that, but it's just the way it is: quoting a US dollar price is a way Saigon vendors often hide their blatant overpricing.

Maybe their goal is to get you to compare with prices back in your country, rather than comparing with prices in Vietnam. For example, $20 for a haircut sounds reasonable if you're coming from a first-world Western country, but it's ridiculous for Vietnam! (Usual Saigon haircut price: 30,000 VND for cheap, 70,000 VND for mid-range, 150,000 VND for fancypants, so about $1 or $3 or $6.)

You should carry and use Vietnamese Dong for everything. Every transaction. Yes, some vendors might accept dollars, but they'll either hate you for it, or they'll build a big exchange markup into the price, or both!

You have two options for getting Vietnamese dong. One option is to use an ATM in Vietnam. Until recently, this was the no-brainer best option. You could withdraw up to 10 million VND (about 500 USD) from many ATMs, with no additional fee (other than what your bank charges). 10 million

VND is a lot of money for hanging out in Vietnam! It's a month's salary for an average Saigonese person.

But nowadays, banks have gotten smarter, or greedier, and the ATM machines often charge a fee of about 50,000 – 100,000 VND to withdraw money, and often have a withdrawal limit of 2 million VND (about $100 USD). So in USD terms, you have to pay 2-5 USD in fees to the ATM (in addition to fees to your own bank back home) every time you withdraw 100 USD! That's a lot of money!

The highest-limit ATMs I know of are HSBC ATMs and they usually have a limit of 10,000,000 VND. That's five times the usual limit of 2,000,000 VND. I particularly recommend the HSBC ATMs at the HSBC bank at the Metropolitan building at 235 Dong Khoi. HSBC ATMs do charge a 200K VND per withdrawal fee. Most other ATMs in Vietnam charge about 50K VND per withdrawal.

I also recommend MB (Military Bank) ATMs, which have ancient software and bad English, but a very reasonable 5,000,000 withdrawal limit.

At any ATM you use (anywhere in the world, actually, not only in Vietnam), always decline the "optional conversion" or the "convenience conversion" or any other such option the ATM gives you. That is the ATM attempting to make money off of you by giving you a bad exchange rate, instead of letting your home bank give you the wholesale exchange rate. Summary: ***decline*** any "optional" service the ATM offers you.

Previous editions of this book recommended using Citibank ATMs. Citibank closed down its Vietnam operations in March 2023, so that advice is no longer relevant.

MY SAIGON: THE LOCAL GUIDE TO HO CHI MINH CITY, VIETNAM

I would also strongly recommend that you only use an ATM that is inside a bank, or attached to a bank. If the ATM eats your card — which is not common, but not unheard of — you will have a heck of a time if the ATM is just standing on a street corner and there's nobody to contact. Vietnamese banks don't shine in customer service. At least if the ATM is inside a bank, you can wave your arms around and make a fuss until somebody makes you fill out a stack of forms and maybe collects a "fee" from you and lets you get your card back.

Oh yeah. And a very Saigonese ATM tip. The day or two before major international soccer matches, ATMs are always out of cash. I'll let you figure out why. I'll just remind you that gambling is a social evil that doesn't exist in Vietnam, and also that in Saigon there are always many motorcycles and phones for urgent sale after a big soccer match.

If you don't want to rely on ATMs, I recommend you bring USD (or Euros or HKD) with you, and change the money here in Saigon. US dollars are the easiest to change, with the best rates. USD is the most popular foreign currency in Saigon. Euros and Hong Kong dollars are close behind – you'll be ok if you bring either one of those. So bring whichever currency is cheapest and easiest for you to obtain.

If you're coming from Asia, it's probably easiest to get HK dollars. If you're coming from Europe, it's probably Euros. Other currencies, like British pounds and Australian and Canadian dollars, can be exchanged, but you should expect more of a price markup, and maybe some difficulty and strange looks when you exchange. So it's better to just stick with US dollars, Euros, or Hong Kong dollars.

There is a well known currency exchange in Saigon, right next to Ben Thanh Market: Mai Van. Its usual customers are the Ben Thanh sellers who accept US dollars – they go change their US dollars to Vietnamese Dong at this shop. You will get the best rates in Saigon at this shop, and you will have no worries about ripoffs or fake money. The only warning about Mai Van: they are closed for lunch every day, around noon until 1 PM.

If you are standing on Le Thanh Ton Street and facing Ben Thanh Market, Mai Van is on the right side. It's outside the west entrance ("cua tay") of Ben Thanh Market. It's at the corner of Nguyen An Minh Street and Phan Chu Trinh Street, but "next to Ben Thanh" is a simpler way to describe its location.

In case Mai Van is closed (it does close for lunch), the shop right across from it, Ha Tam, is also pretty good. It's kind of a Coke or Pepsi thing for Saigonese people; I'm a Mai Van kind of girl, and they are always very kind and very honest with me, but Ha Tam is fine too.

Currency exchanges in Vietnam will give you the best rate only for absolutely new 100 USD bills, ones that look as if they just came off the printing press. Used bills will get a lower rate. Creased bills might not get exchanged at all. And forget about exchanging torn or damaged bills. At least that's the case at those currency exchanges; jewelry shops sometimes will exchange creased, torn, or damaged bills, of course at a significant discount.

An insider tip: the JSC jewelry shop at 174 Le Thanh Ton, just a bit down the street from Mai Van and Ha Tam (look for the big overhead sign that says Agribank), is an excellent alternative if you have a popular currency such as USD or EUR. The jewelry shop is open until 9 or 10 PM most nights, about two hours later than Ha Tam and Mai Van. Also, Ha Tam and Mai Van usually have lines; no lines at JSC jewelry shop, or at most, one or two people in front of you. JSC's rates are usually the same as Mai Van and Ha Tam.

ELLY THUY NGUYEN

Getting around

Saigonese people have motorcycles. You probably don't have one, at least not in Saigon. This sets you apart as a foreigner right away. Yes, Vietnamese people almost always use motorcycles to get around. Walking isn't very popular. According to the World Health Organization, we Vietnamese people walk less than any other country's people! And not many people have private cars, although that is quickly changing, as cars are becoming something for upper-middle-class Saigonese people, not just the really rich. (By the way, imported cars in Vietnam cost about 2-3x what they cost in the US.)

I don't recommend that you rent a motorcycle to try to fit in. Your foreign driving license is not valid in Vietnam, you may be asked to pay huge fines if you are either caught driving without a valid license of or if you are involved in an accident ($20,000 USD to get your passport back from the police if you were involved in an accident — and even if you get a new passport from your embassy, the outgoing immigration police has you on a no-travel list). Saigon traffic is hectic, and it's really not the right place for a casual, fun ride on a motorbike. Yes, many foreigners do rent motorcycles in Saigon. I still don't recommend it. Many foreigners get into major trouble on those same motorcycles.

What about a cyclo, those three-wheeled human-powered contraptions you might've seen in old photos? This might break your heart, but no Saigonese person under the age of eighty ever takes a cyclo. Cyclos were a popular method of transport fifty years ago in Saigon. Nowadays, they're considered dirty and dangerous (can you imagine being on a cyclo that's hit by a car?), and the drivers often scam people. They usually offer you a ride for, say, $1, and then at the end, they (violently) claim that you agreed to pay $100. Bad stuff. I started with that warning because many foreigners assume that Vietnamese people are always taking cyclos everywhere – and that is just totally not true. These days cyclos are about 95% for ripping off tourists and 5% for 90-year-old grandmothers who never found another way to travel.

By the way, if a cyclo driver, or anyone else, tries to extort you, yell as loudly as possible, in English, and make as much of a scene as you can. Those guys will back down. Don't be shy. And don't fall into the pernicious belief that Vietnamese strangers won't help a foreigner. It's usually quite the opposite. I think most Vietnamese people would enjoy getting another Vietnamese person in trouble, especially if it has some justification. (Vietnamese slang lesson: *nem da*, literally "throwing rocks," but usually means something like schadenfreude, enjoying your neighbor's misfortune. Most Vietnamese people will claim that *nem da* is the foundation of Vietnamese culture.)

A Saigonese person who doesn't have a motorcycle usually has three options: a bus, a regular (car) taxi or Grab, or a motorcycle taxi (called "xe om").

Buses are cheap but slow, and I assume that if you are traveling internationally, your vacation time is valuable and you can afford a taxi. Though if you do want to sample a city bus ride in Vietnam, the central bus station is right next to Ben Thanh market. Don't listen to any touts trying to sell you "bus tickets"; the fare, about 9,000 VND, is payable right on the bus. Smoking is banned on buses, but the regulation is ignored and everyone, including the driver, smokes up a storm. Yuck.

Taxis in Saigon used to be generally fine, aside from the few scammers. Nowadays, all the honest taxi drivers have switched to Grab. Basically all that's left among the taxi drivers is the scammers. We Saigonese people don't use taxis anymore, and you shouldn't use them either. That goes for car taxis, and especially for random guys who want to be motorcycle taxis. If you absolutely must use a taxi, Vinasun is the only brand that still has some honest drivers left — but even they aren't that great nowadays. And any brand other than Vinasun is guaranteed to rip you off.

You have to use Grab. Download the app. I covered it in an earlier chapter in this book. You don't need to add a credit card; you can pay with cash. You can order a car or motorcycle from your smartphone. The cars are nicer than taxis, the drivers are more polite, and the rates are lower than taxis'. But, more importantly for a non-Vietnamese person, with Grab, you just type in your destination on your phone, see a fixed fare, and the driver brings you there, without you having to explain anything.

Pro tip: Many Grab drivers are really rural people who have never used a smartphone or GPS and don't really understand the concept of Grab. They think they're driving a taxi. So don't be surprised if they call to ask you your pickup address, yes, the same pickup address you just entered into your app. Just speak English and they'll hang up and get the address from the app. Similarly, don't be surprised if when you get into the car, they want you to tell them the destination. Just point at the Grab app on their phone or yours.

Last pro tip? Why didn't I mention walking? Because outside of the very central part of Q1, walking in Saigon is very dangerous. Seriously. The sidewalks are taken over by motorcycles, and walking on the "sidewalk" is equivalent to walking on a high-speed highway — except with no rules of traffic. Be careful. And as much as I love walking in other cities, in Saigon, keep your walking to the very central area of Q1, or Nguyen Hue walking street (Vietnamese lesson: *pho di bo*, walking street), or one of the city parks.

Eating (way beyond pho)

You've eaten pho back home. You like pho. I know.

But you're in for a shock: in Saigon, we don't eat pho much.

Yes. It's really true.

Of course pho is Vietnamese food, but it's far from being the only Vietnamese food (contrary to what many foreigners think!), and it's a regional specialty of Hanoi. It's not very popular in Saigon. While you can find great pho in Saigon, I really think you should branch out to other foods, especially those that we eat all the time here in Saigon.

Are you still trying to get your head around the idea that we don't eat pho? It's a bit like this. Imagine that you're from the United States. Imagine that a foreign tourist comes to the United States. And imagine that this tourist, back in his home country, has gone to an American Cajun restaurant. And he loves to eat jambalaya at this restaurant. He comes to New York. And in his mind, in America, on every corner, there is a jambalaya restaurant, and Americans are always eating jambalaya – while in fact, jambalaya is just a regional specialty of one specific part of the United States (Louisiana!). Our poor tourist goes around New York, asking for jambalaya in every restaurant, and receiving many confused looks in return.

Is jambalaya American food? Yes, of course. Is jambalaya the only American food? No way.

So when foreigners come to Vietnam thinking that we're always eating pho, it's a lot like this hypothetical tourist coming to America thinking that Americans always eat jambalaya.

ELLY THUY NGUYEN

One neighborhood in Saigon has many pho restaurants. That neighborhood is called Quan Phu Nhuan (Phu Nhuan district). It is the area near the airport, traditionally the area where northerners (Hanoians) live if they move to Saigon.

Now that tourism is growing in Vietnam, Quan 1 (District 1), the central tourist area, also has many pho restaurants, because we Vietnamese people got the memo: foreign visitors want to eat pho! Unfortunately, most of the pho restaurants in District 1 are pretty terrible. They know you're a tourist only here for a few days, so they don't care whether you'll come back to their restaurant.

I've heard of foreigners who visited the pho restaurants in Quan 1 and said that the pho in Vietnam is not as good as the pho back in their home country! Well, you can't really compare, since pho is not Saigonese food, and the restaurants those tourists go to are really just tourist traps, and we Vietnamese people would avoid eating at those places.

So if we don't always eat pho, what do we eat? We eat a lot of rice dishes, especially com tam, which is broken-grained rice with a grilled pork chop on top. We eat noodle soups, such as bun bo hue (spicy beef noodle soup), bun mam (stinky fish-sauce noodle soup), and bun rieu (tomato-sauce noodle soup). We also eat banh xeo (fried pancake), banh uot ("wet noodle," a big white noodle with sauce). As for pho, it's around, but it's not a real Saigonese favorite.

In general, we Saigonese prefer rice, while Hanoians prefer noodles. In fact, it comes through in what we colloquially call our romantic partners. In Saigon slang, your main romantic partner is your rice and your sidepiece is your noodles. (*Com* and *pho*.) And in Hanoi, it's the opposite: your spouse is your

MY SAIGON: THE LOCAL GUIDE TO HO CHI MINH CITY, VIETNAM

pho and your sidepiece is your *com*. And in both Saigon and Hanoi, cultivating backup romantic partners is called *chan rau*, farming vegetables. The more you know!

Ngon and other tourist trap restaurants

Everyone wants to know what are the "best" restaurants in Saigon.

We Vietnamese people love to eat (but doesn't everybody love to eat?), and people get passionate about where to eat the best this and the best that. We sometimes cook at home, but generally less often than in first world countries. "Eating out" is affordable in Vietnam, and not that much more expensive than cooking your own food, so it's not uncommon for someone to never cook at all, and eat all their meals "out."

One thing you'll notice about restaurants in Vietnam is that *all* good restaurants in Vietnam specialize in one dish or small group of dishes. We don't go to a "Vietnamese restaurant" serving all kinds of dishes. We go to a restaurant that specializes in one specific dish, or a couple of dishes. And yes, that means that it's sometimes difficult to decide when eating in a group, because everyone has to agree to eat pretty much the same thing. You will usually see the restaurant's specialty dish advertised on its signboard, sometimes preceded by the words *dac biet*, meaning "house specialty."

There are only two exceptions to this rule of "one restaurant, one dish." One exception is big cafes, which are kind of hangout places, and often serve all kinds of food (often that they literally go buy at a street stall or other restaurant). The cafes want to be meeting places for large groups, and they know that by having a large variety of different foods, they have an advantage over restaurants that might serve just one dish. The other exception is tourist restaurants. If you see a restaurant in Vietnam with a sign in English saying something like "Vietnamese cuisine" or "authentic Vietnamese restaurant," it's a tourist trap. No good restaurant in Vietnam would advertise themselves so vaguely, saying they have "Vietnamese food." So, the first rule: stay away from restaurants that advertise "Vietnamese food."

A particularly flagrant example of Saigon's tourist trap restaurants is the restaurants named Ngon: Nha Hang Ngon (aka Ngon Restaurant), Quan An Ngon, Qua Ngon, and probably a few others with similar Ngon names. They have huge advertising budgets, great central locations, comely (what does that word even mean?) waitresses wearing ao dais, "strong relationships" ($$$) with hotels, guidebooks, and tour operators... and awful food at exorbitant prices.

I think every Vietnam guidebook, other than this one, recommends the Ngon restaurants. Elly is here to tell you to stay away from them, unless you want terrible food at high prices. *Ngon* means "delicious" in Vietnamese, and we Vietnamese people snickeringly refer to these restaurants as *Khong Ngon*, "not delicious."

In general, waitresses dressed in ao dais are a sign of a tourist trap restaurant. Even better: any service staff dressed in ao dais is a sign of a tourist trap. I seriously cannot think of an exception to this rule. Vietnamese people just aren't into their service staff dressed in ao dais. (By the way, it's pronounced *ao yai*, and its history in Vietnam only goes back about a hundred years.)

MY SAIGON: THE LOCAL GUIDE TO HO CHI MINH CITY, VIETNAM

Next, stay away from the Vietnamese restaurants in Pham Ngu Lao, the backpacker district. They are really terribly bad. Often people get stomach-sick at those places.

Actually, there is just one good Vietnamese restaurant in Pham Ngu Lao: Pho Ong Cat Gia at 201 Pham Ngu Lao. It's a 24-hour pho restaurant and it is super delicious. Vietnamese people rag on it because it is "expensive" for Vietnamese standards — it charges about 100K for a bowl of pho, which is twice the usual price — but the quality is worth it, plus it's in a super-expensive location.

If you are stuck in Pham Ngu Lao and want to eat Vietnamese food nearby, my recommendation is either eat Pho Ong Cat Gia, or eat something from a street vendor where you see many Vietnamese people eating, or just go to Highlands Coffee or Trung Nguyen Coffee and eat something they serve there – that will be better than the terrible "Vietnamese restaurants" in Pham Ngu Lao.

Next up on terrible restaurants to always avoid: Pho 24. This is a fast-food restaurant specializing in pho. It's kind of a mystery to us Vietnamese people how this restaurant stays in business, because it is famous for how terrible it is. I have heard that even the employees are scared to eat there!

It has fewer and fewer branches now – when I first wrote this guidebook, Pho 24 had branches all over Saigon, but now they seem to be closing one by one. They still have a strong presence in tourist areas, and most of their customers are tourists.

But anyway, I think you can get better "pho" if you collect some water from a puddle! Sorry, Pho 24! But really, stay away from that place, because it's terrible. (By the way, the original plan for them was to be open 24 hours a day, but they didn't have enough customers for that, so they abandoned that part of the business plan, but kept the name.)

We continue the list of shame, with our next place to avoid: Com Tam Cali. You will see many of these restaurants around Saigon, as they are a chain. They are open pretty late. And com tam is real Saigonese food, unlike pho. Com tam is rice with a pork chop or other meat. Usually the signs will say "Broken rice restaurant." And Com Tam Cali has nice, clean, well-lit restaurants, in prime spaces in Saigon, English menus with clearly indicated prices, and free wifi. Despite all this, the com tam at Com Tam Cali rates about a 2 out of 10 on anyone's food scale. If people eat there, it's either because they're tourists and they don't know better, or just because nothing else is open late at night. Com Tam Cali is bad stuff.

So here's a summary of what restaurants to avoid: Pham Ngu Lao restaurants, the many "Ngon" restaurants (Nha Hang Ngon, Quan An Ngon, Qua Ngon, and others), "Vietnamese restaurant" restaurants, Pho 24, and Com Tam Cali.

Best pho in Saigon

I know you've been waiting for this. I won't stop you from eating pho, and I definitely won't stay quiet (did you expect me to?) about what pho is the best. I just want you to expand your horizons beyond pho. Promise me that you will. And in exchange, here's a list of where you can eat great pho in Saigon.

Pho Hien

269A Nguyen Trai Street, Q1

This is probably the most famous pho restaurant (for Saigonese people!) in Quan 1. It's on Nguyen Trai Street, a street full of clothing shops and all kinds of shopping, so before or after you eat your pho, you can have an interesting look around. They only serve pho with beef, and you will have to choose what kind of beef you want. The good news is that the menu with your beef choices is short, and it's in English! But beware that there's no chicken pho. They do have a "noodles only" pho, which is kind of like a vegetarian dish, but the broth is still made from beef, so it's not really vegetarian.

Pho Le

415 Nguyen Trai Street, Q5

This place is mega-famous with Vietnamese people, but because it's not in Q1, few tourists go there. It's crowded all the time. It does have an English menu, and the staff do speak very basic English, although almost no foreigners eat there. The beef pho is amazing! The only bad thing about it is that it is in Q5, a bit far from the usual tourist environs. It's also on Nguyen Trai Street, near many clothing shops. They used to have another branch on Vo Van Tan, but that closed down during Covid. And there are several fake "Pho Le" restaurants around Saigon; the only real one is at 415 Nguyen Trai.

<u>Huong Binh</u>

148 Vo Thi Sau Street, Q3, near intersection of Vo Thi Sau and Pham Ngoc Thach

This place is at the intersection of Vo Thi Sau and Pham Ngoc Thach. It's just barely in Quan 3, just outside Quan 1. (Actually, some guides mistakenly list it as being in Quan 1.) This restaurant has been in this location for thirty years! My friend's parents dated there! It was featured in a Japanese travel magazine, so nowadays it has quite a few Japanese tourists eating there. And be careful when you walk out of the restaurant, because this is a very busy street, with a lot of traffic. The restaurant is unique on this list because it swings both ways. It serves *both* beef pho and chicken pho. It's the only restaurant on my best pho list that has both types of pho.

For those who prefer chicken pho:

<u>Pho Ga 43</u>

10 Phung Khac Khoan, Q1

Pho Ga 43 doesn't have air conditioning, and it closes at 8 PM, but it has amazing chicken pho. In addition to pho ga (chicken pho), you can get mien ga (thin rice noodles with

MY SAIGON: THE LOCAL GUIDE TO HO CHI MINH CITY, VIETNAM

chicken), chao ga (rice porridge with chicken), or xoi ga (sticky rice... you guessed it, with chicken!). You can ask for "dac biet" for them to throw in extra meat and double the price. Sometimes you gotta splurge. Even the post-doubling price is only about 80K VND, or about $3. Elly tip: if you're super hungry (as I might sometimes be after a late-night writing session, or so I've heard), get *both* pho ga and xoi ga. Skip the cafe sua da the next day and you'll be ok with calories; tell your nutritionist that Elly said so.

<u>Pho Ga Ky Dong</u>
14 Ky Dong, Q 3

This place is a bit far from the central tourist area. It's in a gathering of Hanoian shops and restaurants at 14 Ky Dong, across from the New Pacific Hotel. This restaurant doesn't have a name other than the street name, "Ky Dong." It's like a huge semi-open cafeteria, with tables upon tables under one roof, and everyone chowing down on chicken pho.

Fun bonus: also in the 14 Ky Dong "village" is Bun Oc Thanh Hai, a snail noodle restaurant that in the year 2000 started 14 Ky Dong becoming a northerners' hangout.

Will they secretly serve you dog meat?

You might be scared of being served dog meat if you eat in Saigon. I know the joke. "Welcome to Vietnam. Do you want to eat Fido or Spot?"

A restaurant in Vietnam will never give you dog meat if you ordered something else. Why? Not because they're so nice and ethical. But only because dog meat is *the* most expensive meat in Vietnam, likely much more expensive than whatever you actually ordered. It wouldn't make sense for a restaurant to give you something more expensive than what you paid for.

Actually, Vietnamese people often complain that they ordered and paid for dog meat, but got beef or goat. That is much more likely to happen. As for ordering beef or pork or goat and getting dog – it just doesn't make economic sense from the restaurant's point of view to give you something more expensive than what you paid for.

Additionally, dog meat is rarely served outside specialized dog-meat restaurants, because many Vietnamese people, especially Saigonese people, also hate the idea of eating dogs. Dog is not something that just pops up ho-hum on the menu. It's rare to find a restaurant that serves dog meat that's not an all-out dog meat restaurant.

And generally, the only people who eat dog meat are working-class men from the rural north of Vietnam. I know how classist this sounds, but dog meat just doesn't come up in polite company in Saigon.

Let's talk some more about eating dog meat in Vietnam. In Saigon's northerner-dominated neighborhoods (most well known is the area around the airport) where you see a lot of pho restaurants, you will also see a lot of dog meat restaurants.

The key word to watch for on restaurant signs is *cay*. Cay is dog meat. (But it doesn't always mean that, so don't freak out if you see it somewhere else without context. For example, *cay* in a food context can also mean *spicy*.) You will often see the words "thit cay" or "cay to." You might also see the word *cho*. Same thing. *Cho* is usually the word for a living dog, and *cay* is the word for dog meat, but sometimes *cho* is also used for dog meat.

Dog meat isn't popular among Southern Vietnamese people. Especially among younger people (say, under 40). So if you think the idea of eating dogs is disgusting, your Vietnamese friends might agree with you. Definitely not everyone in Vietnam likes to eat dogs. On the other hand, some southern people, even younger Southern people, do like to eat dog meat. Not all, not most, but some. Almost exclusively men. So you also shouldn't be completely shocked if your new Vietnamese friends, especially men, chow down on Fido. Sorry.

A warning about food allergies

If you have a severe food allergy, such as to peanuts, you may want to think twice about coming to Vietnam.

Food allergies aren't known or taken seriously here. Some anti-science boomer type Westerners come to Vietnam and say, "Look, nobody has peanut allergies in Vietnam, not like those wussy Americans!" Um, yeah, because Vietnamese people with peanut allergies die in childhood.

There's a cause of death in Vietnamese folk medicine called "knocked out by the wind" that's the folk medicine explanation for anaphylactic shock. (Did I ever mention that my dad is a doctor?) Generally less educated Vietnamese people consider it a matter of fate and bad luck, and don't know that "knocked out by the wind" is caused by specific allergies and is preventable and treatable.

Even if you try to explain to street food vendors or restaurants that you have an allergy to an ingredient, it's very likely that they won't take it seriously, and anyway, all the ingredients are mixed together during preparation, and they use the same surfaces and utensils and so on.

Expensive high-end hotel restaurants (think Park Hyatt) are going to be better about this, but do you really want to be coming to Vietnam to have $20/plate Hyatt dishes for every meal?

So if your food allergies are mild enough that they're just a mild annoyance, bring lots of antihistamines and Epipens and whatever else you use to manage them, and don't expect anyone to really understand and care for them — most everything touches peanuts (a very popular ingredient here) or shellfish or any number of other things.

If your food allergies are life-threatening, I would ask you to seriously reconsider whether you really want to come here, or to eat nothing but food you buy from the grocery store or from expensive hotel restaurants.

Sorry.

What's a typical Saigonese meal?

I already told you many times in this book that we don't eat pho at every meal. And I told you that no matter what your friends who heard about your trip to Vietnam told you, we don't eat Fido for every meal! So what would be a typical South Vietnamese meal?

One of the most common South Vietnamese meals is com tam. That literally means "broken rice." But the real meaning of com tam is that it's small-grained rice served with meat. It's typically served with a pork chop. Sometimes, in addition to or instead of the pork chop, you also get some sliced sausage, a fried egg, or a pork cake (kind of like a slice of bologna).

The history of com tam is that when Vietnam was a very poor country, we Vietnamese people could only afford to eat the "defective" rice, the broken grains. We had to export all the "good" rice. Nowadays, we can afford to eat the "good" rice (and lots of it, as I'm reminded every time I weigh myself), but we still have a passion for "com tam" cuisine.

Another typical South Vietnamese meal is vegetable or fish broth (often called "canh") that's served with a bowl of rice. This style of meal also comes from the times when Vietnam was poorer. Each person at the table (Vietnamese people traditionally eat in family groups) has a bowl of rice, and everyone just pours a bit of the broth on their rice to flavor their rice. These days, the bowls of soup are bigger than the bowls of rice, and the soup has more meat, fancier vegetables, and less broth! But still, we eat "canh," broth, with rice. It's an especially popular lunch meal.

And, despite my lecturing you about pho, we do eat a lot of noodles! Just not in pho. We commonly eat "hu tieu," which are flat noodles, and "bun," "mi," and "mien," all of which are thin noodles.

Bun is doughy white noodles. Mi is yellow Chinese-style egg noodles. Mien is see-through clear rice flour noodles.

Usually you will see restaurant or shop or menu signs with the name of one of these noodles, sometimes together with a type of meat or preparation. We'll cover the basic food words a bit later.

There's a good place for you to try a very typical (in the best sense of the word) home-cooking-style Saigonese meal. It's about as home-cooked Saigonese as it gets.

It's Cafe Bang Khuang, at the top of the old apartment building at 9 Thai Van Lung in Q1. (Make sure you go to the top floor! There are fake imitators of Bang Khuang on the lower floors, most notoriously a place called Nguoi Saigon.) Bang Khuang is a nice cafe, but it's most popular as an office workers' lunch spot, between around 11 and 2. Again, no pho, but lots of home-cooked style Vietnamese lunch dishes and there's a menu in English.

For dinner, I suggest com tam – rice with a pork chop, very quintessentially Saigonese, though sometimes considered too heavy for lunch, so more popular as either a breakfast or dinner meal. The best and most famous com tam in Saigon is at Com Tam Ba Ghien at 84 Dang Van Ngu in Quan Phu Nhuan, not far from the airport. Glorious grilled pork chops. There's even a picture menu on the wall. The basic question is what you want on your rice; choose one or two or five of these:

MY SAIGON: THE LOCAL GUIDE TO HO CHI MINH CITY, VIETNAM

suon, grilled pork chop (everyone gets this, but the waitresses will assume foreigners are weird, so you may need to specifically tell them that you want this)
ga, chicken, usually chicken wing
lap xuong, sausage
op la, sunny-side-up egg
bi, shredded pork skin (FYI: Elly hates)
cha lua, a bologna-like thing

Chuyen Ky: traditional Saigonese food

I've told you many times that pho isn't really Saigonese food. Com tam, in the previous section, really is one example of Saigon food.

As a rule of thumb, in Vietnam, Saigonese people prefer rice, and Hanoians prefer noodles. In fact, there's dating/relationship slang along these lines. In Saigon, your primary romantic partner is (in slang) called your rice, and your sidepiece is called your noodles. I'm not making this up. And in Hanoi, it's the reverse.

So where's the rice? Well, one very traditional and very well-regarded old (cough, pre-1975, cough) Saigonese restaurant is called Chuyen Ky. It serves a very fragrant type of rice that's been steamed in a bowl, with various dishes to go along with it. It's been famous since the 1940s, and it's actually near the Ton That Dam hipster apartment building I've described.

The main thing you want to get at Chuyen Ky is either rice with beef and sausage (*com bo lap xuong*) or rice with chicken (*com ga*). Then add on some soup (*canh*). The bowls of rice cost about 60K VND, which is pretty expensive (quality, history, location), and they're small enough so you should get one or even two per person. Then the soup is a big dish, so you can get one to share for a few people.

This is very classic Saigonese food! This place is also Instagrammable, in that dilapidated-old-restaurant kind of way.

Chuyen Ky is at 65 Ton That Dam in Q1 and it's open 11 AM until 9 PM. The menu on the table is all in Vietnamese, but when I asked about English, they said they do have an English menu, but they couldn't find it right at that moment so couldn't show it to me. They also speak Cantonese, but I'm not confident enough of my mad Cantonese skillz to extensively test that.

By the way, there will be some naysayers, usually know-it-all foreigners, who will say, "Nuh-uh, Chuyen Ky isn't authentic Saigon food, because it's Cantonese!"

These are the same people who will tell you, "Nuh-uh, a slice of pizza isn't authentic New York City food, because it's Italian!" Just ignore them.

Saigonese breakfast on a hot plate

You might have heard that "Vietnamese people eat pho for breakfast." That's kind of true. Pho is indeed primarily a breakfast dish, but it's more of a northern thing, not a Saigon thing.

A very Saigonese breakfast is, instead, banh mi chao. Yes, there's a baguette, as you might be used to with *banh mi*. But the usual way to serve banh mi chao is with a frying pan full of eggs, sausage, cheese, and other breakfast stuff — and the baguette on the side. You eat it sitting down, usually directly from the frying pan. You can also ask for the contents of the frying pan to be put inside your baguette, but this is a less popular option, especially because there's too much stuff (or should be too much stuff!) in that frying pan to fit inside a baguette.

Banh mi chao places are open only in the morning. The most famous banh mi chao in Saigon is Banh Mi Hoa Ma at 53 Cao Thang in Q3 (6AM-11AM). This is the oldest breakfast restaurant in Saigon. It also claims to have invented banh mi sandwiches, when its regular customers didn't have time to sit down and eat.

It's a small and crowded shop, and you'll probably have to sit outside, with motorcycles and construction equipment zooming by. The waitstaff are pretty busy, so they might not seem friendly. They're nice, just overworked.

But actually, I don't think Banh Mi Hoa Ma is that great for taste, and especially for price and value. It's a bit expensive (60K or so) and their food isn't outstanding. It's good, not great.

There's recently been a very popular newcomer to Saigon's banh mi chao game: Banh Mi Chao Co Le, also known as Banh Mi Bue Due. I think this place is the best banh mi chao going. If you search YouTube for "banh mi bue due," you'll find that every Vietnamese food vlogger gushes over this place, though it hasn't appeared in English-language guidebooks — until now.

Remember that slang term for homosexuality, bue due? Yeah. That term. I asked the owner why she calls it that, and she said something about two eggs and sausage, and therefore bue due. I don't know. (The name is probably also a response to the sandwich place on Le Thi Rieng known as "lesbian banh mi.")

It's a small stand, not a full restaurant. You can eat on tiny stools on the street, usually populated by crowds of teenagers from the nearby high school, or get your frying pan inside a baguette, to go. Like most banh mi chao places, it's open 6AM-11AM.

MY SAIGON: THE LOCAL GUIDE TO HO CHI MINH CITY, VIETNAM

• • • •

Your options are with or without sausage, sardines, and cheese. The price is 30K or 35K, depending on what fillings you choose and how much she likes you. I think her secret here is she loads her food with sea salt. It's salty. And delicious.

It's a bit difficult to find, but the location in Google Maps is accurate. It's the small stand outside Lo E (building E) in the cluster of old apartment buildings down the alley at 213 Nguyen Thien Thuat. A car can't get you all the way to the stand, so get out at 213 Nguyen Thien Thuat and walk the rest of the way. Note that there are a few fakes (because of course there are) when you're on the way there: they are usually called "Co [something]" that's not Co Le (the real one).

And tell her Elly says hi.

If you don't want to leave the central Saigon area, or if it's already past 11 AM, you have another option: a very centrally located banh mi chao place that's open until late evening. It doesn't really have a name, but it's on the Nguyen Hue main walking street in Q1, between Oscar Hotel and Nguyen Thiep street, near 72 Nguyen Hue. They have a juice bar for foreigners and a banh mi chao place for Vietnamese people. The taste here is not nearly as good as Co Le / Bue Due, but it's not bad.

MY SAIGON: THE LOCAL GUIDE TO HO CHI MINH CITY, VIETNAM

Where to hang out in Saigon?

Where do "the locals" (that's the word Lonely Planet always uses) hang out in Saigon? There's basically only one answer, other than the silly answers like "at home": at cafes. The cafe culture is huge in Saigon. It's like Starbucks in other countries, but times a million!

Need to meet your friends? Need to work? Need to pick up girls/guys? Need to eat? Need to take a nap? Need to pee? Need some free air conditioning? Go to a cafe!

If you want a sample of Saigon cafe life, just walk around the vicinity of your hotel and walk into any cafe you might find. Look for signs that say "Cafe" or signs that say "Trung Nguyen" or "Highlands" – though Trung Nguyen and Highlands are chain cafes that are a little bit more like Starbucks and a little bit less like the traditional Vietnamese cafe experience.

Assuming you're in a traditional Vietnamese cafe, when you walk in, scope out a table for sitting. A waitress might approach you and ask you how many people, and you can hold up one or two or ten fingers. And find a table that has a good view of the people and everything else that's going on. Also watch out for cigarette smoke – unfortunately, we still have cigarette smoking in cafes in Vietnam, although it's officially illegal.

Order yourself a coffee, either by talking to the waitress or pointing at the menu. You should basically say one of two things: "cafe sooa" (cafe sua), which means cafe with milk, or "cafe den," which means black coffee. You can also say "da" for ice or "nong" for hot. (Many cafe waitresses in the tourist area now know to say "cold" or "hot," so you might hear that too.)

Do not. Do not. DO NOT order a latte or cappuccino in a traditional, old-fashioned Vietnamese cafe! I know that's what you order in Starbucks in your country. But 99.9% of old-fashioned Vietnamese cafes (I'm not talking about the new hipster "specialty coffee / third wave" places, so relax) don't know how to make those drinks.

In the past, before Vietnam became popular for Western tourists, cafes had probably never heard of those drinks. Now, they might have lattes and cappuccinos on their menus, just for tourists. But don't order them. They're terrible. All my foreign friends who ordered them were disappointed, or sometimes disgusted. In old-fashioned Vietnamese cafes, should stick to the regular Vietnamese drinks, like cafe sua da (iced coffee with milk).

Then the fun begins! Along with your coffee, you'll get a glass of water or weak iced tea. That is refilled for free. You are not expected to drink your coffee right away when you get it. This is not an Italian espresso bar where people stay for thirty seconds on their way somewhere. You're expected to spend at least an hour drinking that coffee! Or longer. And sip that iced water and tea after you're done with your coffee drink. Watch people. Use wifi on your phone or laptop. Smile at any attractive people of whatever gender interests you!

When I originally wrote this book in 2013, the trend among Saigon cafes was over-the-top luxury: who could have the plushest sofas, the fanciest wall paintings, the biggest sound system, and the fastest wifi. Now the trend has changed, and the new fashion among Saigon cafes is minimalism, in the form

MY SAIGON: THE LOCAL GUIDE TO HO CHI MINH CITY, VIETNAM

of little wooden stools in open-air fashion. (That is actually a Hanoian way of drinking coffee! Props to our Northern compatriots... I think!) Many formerly luxurious cafes have converted into the minimalist style.

The other cafe fashion now, perhaps replacing "minimalist cafes," is "vintage cafes," usually focusing on collecting "vintage" stuff, real or fake, usually vintage meaning 1970s or so. These cafes also like dim lighting, and often pride themselves on being physically difficult to find, with unmarked doors.

There's one actually vintage, actually old cafe you should visit. It's not willfully, stylized vintage. It's just old. It was founded in 1938 and has been more or less operating continuously (cough cough except for a while after the 1975 invasion cough cough) since then. It's the oldest cafe in Saigon!

It's called Cheo Leo. The name means "bluff" or "cliffside," because originally, in 1938, that area looked like a bluff or cliffside. It's at 109/36 Nguyen Thien Thuat. That means it's house #36 on the alley at 109 Nguyen Thien Thuat. An easy way to get there is to go to 130 Ly Thai To. The alley at 130 Ly Thai To is actually the alley of 109 Nguyen Thien Thuat. Or just go to the address 109 Nguyen Thien Thuat and start walking down the alley until you see house 36 on your right. I know it sounds confusing, but it will make sense when you're there. And you can also use Google Maps to find it.

Cheo Leo operates on an old-fashioned schedule: 6:00 AM until 6:00 PM, and closed on the second and fifteenth days of every month. They make coffee using a "sock" (kind of like Malaysian coffee), not using the French-style press filters. And everything is really, really cheap. The lovely grandmas who run the place run it to honor their father who founded it in 1938, and they're not doing it for the money.

I used to be able to say there are no tourists at Cheo Leo, but nowadays, guided Saigon tours do often stop there. The other customers are a mix of salty old men (hooray!), college-aged hipsters, and nearby office workers.

Then there's "new vintage." New vintage cafes are actually not old, but try to fashion themselves in a retro style. Some examples of "new vintage" are Cafe ID at 61B Tu Xuong in Q 3, Collector Cafe at 46 Nguyen Van Trang (just off of Nguyen Trai) in Q1, Cafe Vintage at 23 Tu Xuong in Q3, and Cafe Nguoi Saigon on the second floor of the old apartment building at 9 Thai Van Lung (corner of Thai Van Lung and Nguyen Sieu).

Cafe Vintage is cool because it really feels like a secret place – it's just an unmarked door in a semi-residential neighborhood. Note that they don't allow you to use electronics after 6 PM.

Cafe Nguoi Saigon is an ode to pre-1975 Saigon. There's a wall mural depicting not just the physical appearance and the fashions of pre-1975 times, but even the slang used then. It is interesting in itself that this place is allowed to operate; some ten years ago, running such a cafe would have landed the owners in prison. Maybe enough years have passed so that reminiscing about pre-1975 Saigon is no longer threatening. Maybe. No matter what the political undercurrents, Cafe Nguoi Saigon may currently be the most fashionable cafe in Saigon. Celebrities are fond of posting selfies of themselves on the cafe's balcony. I recommend you try the balcony too, whether or not you're a celebrity. Minus points because Cafe

MY SAIGON: THE LOCAL GUIDE TO HO CHI MINH CITY, VIETNAM

Nguoi Saigon rips off Cafe Bang Khuang, which is physically above it; actually, both are worth a visit.

Cafe ID is perhaps the inventor of the vintage cafe concept. It just moved to a new location, as its old landlord wanted to open his own vintage cafe at their old location.

Saigon cafe fashion is always changing. Maybe next year, the new trend will be cafe swimming pools or waiters on roller skates or upside-down seating *(update: there is now actually a cafe with upside-down furniture installed on the ceiling – Up Cafe on Nguyen Trong Tuyen in Phu Nhuan)*. You read it here first *(update: yes indeed you did!)*.

That's Saigon cafe fashion, the forefront of style and what's going on. For now, the epitome of the current fashion for "minimalist" cafes is Cafe Vy, at the corner of Le Thanh Ton and Le Anh Xuan, while the epitome of "vintage" cafes is Nguoi Saigon, upstairs at the corner of Thai Van Lung and Nguyen Sieu.

That brings me to another point I wanted to talk about, and one maybe many of my readers will be interested in: how to score chicks! Or dudes. Or whatever you like.

How to score chicks in Vietnam

I literally wrote a book literally called *Dating Vietnamese Women*. The deep-dive details are there. But I'll give you a summary here.

Here's the bad news. Vietnam is not like the West. People go to bars in Vietnam in groups to hang out with their friends they already know. They don't go to meet new people. And talking to random strangers in public is considered super-creepy in Vietnam.

The only way you will meet new women in a bar in Vietnam is if 1) You are a model or a celebrity or have a million-dollar-plus car parked outside the bar door or 2) Those women are friends of your friends or 3) Those women are prostitutes. Sorry, there are pretty much no exceptions to those rules. (Actually, there's been a recent trend in Saigon that does create an exception – that woman could be selling Amway or Herbalife! These days many people, especially good-looking young women, go to bars and cafes to chat up strangers and try to enroll them into multilevel marketing. This isn't a business advice book, but I advise you to steer clear of such "opportunities.")

Maybe the closest thing to an exception to these rules will be for #3, some of those women might not be hourly-money-for-sex prostitutes, but they look for money in return for sex: something like one guy to pay her rent and one guy to buy her a phone and one guy to pay for her new motorbike. They're still pretty much prostitutes.

And the same is mostly true for meeting guys too, whether you're a hetero girl looking to meet hetero guys or a gay guy looking to meet gay guys. Vietnamese people just don't go out meeting strangers in bars or cafes. We just don't do that.

Although I know Vietnamese guys, straight and gay alike, who approach foreign tourists in bars and chat them up, purely in hopes of a one-night stand. These male friends of mine know that Westerners, unlike us Vietnamese people, consider it normal for strangers to talk to them in bars. So maybe if you're looking for guys, there's some chance of a one-night stand with no strings attached in Saigon. Even then, be wary of anyone who tries to make fast friends with you. My good-time-seeking male friends are after nothing more than a night (or three) of pleasure and aren't going to rob or extort anybody, but I can't guarantee the same of other men who try to chat you up.

And if you're a single guy (sorry, I talk about guys because usually foreign guys are much more interested in dating in Vietnam than foreign girls are), you can assume that any woman who "hits on you" in a bar or similar place is up to no good. Maybe she wants cash, or maybe she's trying to recruit for Herbalife, or maybe she wants someone to pay for her drug habit, or maybe worse, like her boyfriend is waiting around the corner to rob you. Be careful, because women "hitting on" men is absolutely outside the norm of Vietnamese culture.

But there's good news. A lot of it. If you're a single guy, you can easily chat with university students, hotel receptionists, cafe waitresses, shop clerks, most any woman, and many will be interested in you. Exchange Facebook IDs or Viber or Wechat IDs (Whatsapp is used only by the elite here) and chat away, maybe with the help of Google Translate.

MY SAIGON: THE LOCAL GUIDE TO HO CHI MINH CITY, VIETNAM

Girls like that often speak some English. They will be happy to spend some time with you. They will love to be called your girlfriend. These are the regular girls, usually from the countryside of Vietnam, from families of modest means (or even less), who would love to have a foreign boyfriend. Exactly how to deal with them is a big separate topic I wrote a whole book about (again, please see *Dating Vietnamese Women,* by highly acclaimed, world-renowned author Elly Thuy Nguyen), but I can give you some basic tips here.

The biggest tip is that simpler, less worldly Vietnamese people (that means the girls talking to you in a cafe or mall) overestimate how wealthy and prosperous foreigners are. Many less educated Vietnamese women, of the kind who will try to chat you up, firmly believe that every foreign man has a few million dollars in his bank account, as a *minimum*, and that he easily spends several thousand dollars every day. Really, this is what they think you can offer them.

Simpler Vietnamese people believe that the basic financial difference between Vietnam and the first world is that the Vietnamese currency is worth so little. So when a minimum-wage salary in Saigon might be five million dong a month (about $220), they believe that a minimum-wage salary in the first world might be five million dollars or Euros or pounds a month. Not joking. I would say that more than half of average, rural Vietnamese people believe that.

And if the average is five million dollars a month, well, if this guy is traveling abroad, he must be especially rich, so he's probably raking in at least ten million dollars a month! No joke. That's what they think.

Hey, if you came from rural poverty, and no rich Vietnamese guy would consider you as a wife because you're a "rural hick," and now you have a chance to date a guy who earns ten million dollars a month — wouldn't you be excited? I mean, even if you're a guy who doesn't swing that way, wouldn't you at least pretend— ok, I'm getting a bit far afield.

The point is, they, the simple cafe or retail-clerk girls who approach you have dreams. Lots of dreams. Unrealistic ones. Expectations that, unless you really do rake in ten million dollars a month (what's up, Jay-Z), you probably can't fulfill. So be careful. Vietnamese women's needs and requests might be way beyond what you'd expect, and you might be setting everyone up for heartbreak.

Maybe it's also because they see stories about celebrities, or they watch movies, or they hear exaggerated stories from their friends or their friends' boyfriends. These women might have very unrealistic expectations about what you can bring them.

She might think that once she is your girlfriend, you buying houses and cars for her and her family is pocket change for you – because remember, you spend several thousand dollars every day, and you regularly take a million dollars out of the ATM! After all, a Vietnamese person spends several thousand dong every day, and regularly takes a million dong out of the ATM, and you earn and spend USD, so why not?

Of course, more highly educated and more worldly Vietnamese women know that most foreigners aren't rich, and will generally have more realistic ideas of first-world Westerners. But those same more educated and more worldly Vietnamese women are also generally not that interested in foreign guys, unless the foreign guy is special, or she really

MY SAIGON: THE LOCAL GUIDE TO HO CHI MINH CITY, VIETNAM

likes him, or whatever hoops you might have to jump through back in your own country in order for a woman to like you. I don't think that's a coincidence. More worldly Vietnamese women see you realistically, and you have to appeal to them realistically, not through a fantasy of millions of dollars raining down upon her village every day.

I promised you another warning. So this other warning is that many Vietnamese couples consider each other boyfriend-girlfriend for years, and never have sex. I know that in most Western cultures, calling one another boyfriend-girlfriend implies you're having sex. Not so in Vietnam. Of course many Vietnamese women have sex before marriage, but it's more common for a long term couple who have plans of marrying, not for someone you've known for a week.

Now, of course, you might meet lots of Vietnamese women, some of them not even straight-up prostitutes, who are willing to have sex with you after just a few dates. But you should know that this is *not* the norm. So you should ask yourself: why is this woman acting outside the Vietnamese norm? Maybe she is a prostitute. Maybe. Or maybe she has some plans you don't know about. Or maybe she's been rejected by her Vietnamese peers or husband. Or maybe she has lots of other guys she calls "boyfriend" at the same time as you. Just be careful!

By the way: in Vietnamese culture, even among younger people, even now, being boyfriend-girlfriend is seen as only a lead-up to marriage and procreation. There's no other purpose.

Vietnamese people will be puzzled if you say that someone is your boyfriend or girlfriend but you have no plans of marrying them. To Vietnamese people – yes, even younger people! – being boyfriend and girlfriend is the same as being engaged to marry. And breaking up is taken as seriously as breaking off an engagement to marry: which is to say, of course it does happen, but it's a big deal! So be careful when you let any girl say that you are her boyfriend!

Try talking with the store clerks in big shopping malls, like Vincom Center or Crescent or Parkson. Try talking with cafe waitresses. Try talking with the women who cut your hair.

Just remember that if a woman works in Q1, and she speaks some English, she is always meeting many, many foreign guys, so she is likely chatting with lots of other guys just as she's chatting with you! And even if she says she's "single," that can have some pretty flexible meanings. Almost all of the young women who come from the countryside to work in Saigon have their boyfriends back in the countryside (or who came to Saigon together with them to work), even if they deny it to you.

But there's another way to meet chicks. Try online. Facebook is huge in Vietnam, especially Facebook groups. You should do this a few weeks or even months before you actually come to Vietnam, so you can have some conversations and establish some friendships. Even if you don't meet the love of your life, it might be fun to have some Vietnamese friends, of any gender, to go hang out with. We do love to meet foreigners.

Tinder? In Vietnam, it's considered almost entirely a gold-digger app, and every man on Tinder, Vietnamese or foreign, mostly flaunts his wealth. I don't think that's a good way to build a real relationship, but if you want to splash some cash and date a "hotgirl" (that is actually Saigonese slang), go for it.

And lastly, I know many foreigners use vietnamcupid.com. Here on the Vietnamese side, it's seen as kind of a last-ditch refuge for older, rural Vietnamese women desperate to get married ASAP. That might be good or bad for you.

Anyway, you'll have no problem finding lots of Vietnamese women online, and you can at least meet them for a cafe chat when you come to Vietnam.

If you're not too far outside the college age range, you can try talking with the college students who hang around 9-23 park (the park between Ben Thanh Market and Pham Ngu Lao) looking for English conversation partners. While you shouldn't assume any girl who talks to you there wants to date you, and you should remember that you're not the first handsome foreigner she's ever seen, it might be an enjoyable experience for you to chat to some Vietnamese college students, at least if you're not so old that it would be creepy. (How old is that? You can decide for yourself! But keep in mind that as much as you see elderly white men with young Vietnamese women around Saigon, that is not considered normal in Vietnamese culture, and university students are less inclined to engage in such relationships than farm girls and prostitutes are.)

Scam warning: There's a recent scam involving "attractive Vietnamese women" approaching foreign male tourists online (often on dating apps) or in person, and inviting them on a date (often with hints at sex) at a specific place, often a bar. Once you're at the bar, your "date" will order a few drinks, then "get an emergency phone call from her mother" and have to rush out, and you'll be asked to pay "the bill for her drinks" — something like $1,000 USD, or whatever they think they can extort from you. There will be thugs to extort you. They may also drug your drink. If you're reading this, you probably know well enough to avoid this scam, but if it does happen to you, I suggest you pay with your credit card, then once they let you go, immediately call your credit card company and dispute the charge.

Gay Saigon

There's no specific "gay neighborhood" or "gay street" in Saigon. But there's a huge gay scene. And thanks to my extensive network of gay friends, classmates, and colleagues, I'm giving you the lowdown.

First, and quite importantly, homosexuality is not and never has been illegal in Vietnam. That makes Vietnam different from most Asian countries.

Gay marriage is semi-legal here. It was un-banned, although gay married couples still don't receive full marriage recognition. In practice, everything depends on who you know and how much cash you can give them — it's still Vietnam! Still, any acceptance of gay marriage is pretty amazing for a communist Southeast Asian country, isn't it? Hooray, Vietnam!

A common scam played on gay tourists to Saigon is some street thug threatening to "report them" unless they pay blackmail money. There's nothing to report. Legally speaking, no one in Vietnam cares if you're gay, or if you just had gay sex with someone. Socially speaking, no one in Saigon cares that you're gay. Younger, more urban people even welcome and celebrate it.

Unfortunately, the atmosphere is much less gay-friendly in Vietnam outside Saigon. So, hooray, Saigon!

Despite the oft-cited Kinsey statistic of ten percent, way more than ten percent of the guys you see around central Saigon will be blatantly, showing-off gay, and who knows how many more are gay but don't show it off. The common belief – which makes good sense to me – is that all the gay people from everywhere in Vietnam move to Saigon, because it's the only place in Vietnam where homosexuality is accepted. If you meet someone in Saigon and they "seem gay" to you (whatever that means!), you might very well be right.

On the other hand, in rural Vietnam, it is common for same-gender friends to hold hands, walk down the street arm-in-arm, and even play with each other's hair or rub each other's backs. As far as they're concerned, there's nothing gay about it. And in traditional, rural Vietnamese culture, there's nothing gay about one man telling another man how handsome he is. That's changing, but only slowly.

I remember the story told by my high school teacher, a heterosexual American man. When he first started working in Vietnam, his male Vietnamese colleague put his arm around him, put his head on his shoulder, and told him, "You're the most handsome man I've ever seen." My American teacher was certain there was a misunderstanding. I'm not delusional when I tell you there was nothing gay intended by his Vietnamese colleague.

Now as for people who are actually gay? Gay couples (mostly male) are easy to spot anywhere in Saigon. They might even engage in some man-on-man PDA. No one really minds. My friend works in a well-known financial firm in Saigon and

MY SAIGON: THE LOCAL GUIDE TO HO CHI MINH CITY, VIETNAM

estimates that more than half of her male banker colleagues are openly gay.

At least at the level of casual strangers on the street, no one cares. If you start getting closer to people, then sure, some homophobia might come up, especially among older people.

To the extent that I'm a typical college-educated millennial Saigonese woman, I have gay male friends and that's not uncommon – although straight Vietnamese men might be more hesitant to be friends with openly gay men. And of course, if you're coming out to your family, or if you're in a position of authority, it might be difficult, as it might be anywhere in the world. But insofar as you're probably not marrying into any Vietnamese families or getting a job in Vietnam, this shouldn't be a concern for you.

The usual word for gay is just *gay* in Vietnamese. The older word, now in less common use, is *pe de*, which, unfortunately, comes from the French slang for a pedophile – although Vietnamese people use that term without knowing that it refers to pedophilia. And bisexuality is traditionally called *hai phai*, which sounds just like the English term "hi fi," and literally means bidirectional, but nowadays people just say *bi*. (Vietnamese slang lesson: The archaic and homophobic term *pe de* is out of favor, but nowadays young people slur the old slur, and lovingly refer to gay people as *bue due* — and the more you stretch that out, the better, so *buueee duuueeeee* if you're being cute.)

Many gay guys looking to meet foreign gay men go to 9/23 park, the park I recommend for meeting Vietnamese college students, the Nguyen Hue walking area, or just about anywhere in Pham Ngu Lao. Hookups happen in the evenings in most big public gyms and public swimming pools around central Saigon. Use your imagination (or don't) for that part. And of course all the gay dating apps are popular, especially Grindr and Blued.

The famous cafe hangouts for gay people are Pride Cafe at 166 Tran Hung Dao and Secret Garden at 158 Pasteur in Quan 1. There's also Manfolk at 69 (I'm not making this up) Nguyen Thi Minh Khai, although Manfolk gets a few stars deducted for allowing smoking.

All of these places are not exclusively gay (don't assume everyone there is gay), but they're heavily gay populated. Also, the hipster cafes in the section of this book dedicated to them will always be heavily gay populated, even if they're not exclusively or maybe not even majority gay.

The most famous bar/club type hangout for gay men into the club scene is Frolic Bar at 151 De Tham in Pham Ngu Lao. You can find a ton about it if you Google. It's famous and I almost feel as if I don't need to tell my gay readers about Frolic Bar because all gay people worldwide already know about it (I know that's stupid and I'm stereotyping, but indulge me please!).

What else? There's gay life everywhere in Saigon. If you're a gay couple, older, rural people will most likely think you're good same-sex friends, but younger, urban people will know what's up. It won't be a problem.

Who are those young women in tight clothes?

Around Saigon's tourist areas, there are some hair salons and massage shops where young women wear tight, skimpy clothes, and stand on the street asking tourists walking by if they'd like to come inside for a massage.

What do you think is going on in these establishments?

If you think what I think you think, you're wrong.

It's funny how these places prominently advertise massage. Because you're supposed to think "wink wink, massage, *if you know what I mean*." And they want you to think there's going to be more than just a massage. And pay a lot of money and have big expectations. But here's the problem: it's only a massage!

So I'm going to tell you now: there's no prostitution or "extra services" at these salons, unless by "extra services" you mean a manicure.

The whole trick of these "pretty girl" hair salons and massage shops is to trade on Vietnam's unfortunate reputation as a hotbed of prostitution and get tourists to pay a lot of money and think there's going to be sex inside. But there's no sex inside. It's like Chris Rock says: "There's no sex in the Champagne Room!"

Of course you're welcome to flirt and chat with the employees, as they flirt with dozens of customers every day. And they'll demand some pretty big tips from you (maybe five hundred thousand VND for a hair wash and a quick back rub).

But don't expect anything more than exactly what is advertised: hair shampoo and a massage.

Yes, there is prostitution in Vietnam. But this isn't it.

And I really don't want to be advising you on where to find prostitution in Vietnam. But if this were really a prostitution joint, it would be an unmarked door down some back alley, there'd be a gangster hanging around protecting it, and the women working there would be too ashamed to be standing out on the street advertising. Vietnam isn't Thailand, and any place with women standing out on the street pulling you in isn't actual prostitution.

Actual Vietnamese prostitution is full of gangsters and human trafficking, and foreigners get ripped off when trying to get prostitutes in Vietnam – not ripped off like overcharged, but ripped off like being given sleeping pills and being robbed. So I recommend you stay away from it.

The wacky tobacky

"Marijuana? Want some marijuana?"

You'll likely hear that spoken advertisement by some dude riding alongside you on a motorcycle if you are a non-Vietnamese person, especially under forty years old, walking around anywhere in central Saigon.

It's my warning that you shouldn't get involved in this. Not just because smoking is bad for you, but because this is almost always a scam. You'll be robbed, or you'll be sold some regular tobacco cigarettes, but, most commonly, you'll be turned in to the police, who pay a commission to these street drug dealers to turn you in. In fact, Vietnamese people have a funny saying about these "drug deals," saying it's tea money (a bribe the tourist must pay to the police) for tea (fake marijuana, usually tea) that the tourist was sold.

Nowadays, this marijuana scam is becoming more popular on Facebook, especially in Facebook groups for foreigners in Vietnam. A lot of scammers claim to be selling marijuana through Facebook, and of course require prepayment. You won't be getting any marijuana from them. The best you can hope for is the scammers just take your money and leave you alone. The worst is that the police will knock on your door.

Drugs in Vietnam, even "only" marijuana, are a very serious thing. It's not like the Western world where it's "only" marijuana and you get a slap on the wrist if anything at all. In Vietnam, if you are caught by the police with one marijuana cigarette, it's no different from being caught with a suitcase full of cocaine. It's not seen any differently. It's a big crime. And it's going to take either a big long trial, and intervention by your embassy, or maybe a significant "donation" (at least $10,000 USD), to get you out of trouble. So don't do it, please!

That said – of course many younger Vietnamese people like smoking marijuana. And I know some Vietnamese grandpas who fondly remember the plentiful marijuana in Saigon brought in by US soldiers during the 1960s and 1970s. The Vietnamese word for marijuana is *can sa*, a Vietnamization of the word *ganja*.

You can sometimes smell or see marijuana being smoked in some of Saigon's youth-oriented cafes and bars. But it's not as common as in the West. And it's still very illegal. So if you start hanging out with college-aged Vietnamese people, you might encounter marijuana. But not nearly as often as in the West. And I really advise you not to get into anything illegal on your vacation.

Where to hang out in cafes

Here are some Saigon cafes you can try. This is where Vietnamese people go, but you won't feel really out of place there as a foreigner – although you will likely be the only foreigner there, because these places aren't on the usual tourist path.

All these cafes are in central Saigon, so they are close to where you'll stay. When are they open? Unfortunately, for Vietnamese cafes, the opening times vary a bit, sometimes depending on the season or the day of week or how well the economy is doing and how late people stay out, or sometimes even based on the weather! In general, you can expect cafes to be open about 7AM until 9PM. (Yes, Vietnamese establishments generally don't stay open late.)

<u>Cafe Vy</u>

277 Le Thanh Ton, Q1 (Corner of Le Anh Xuan Street and Le Thanh Ton Street, next to New World Hotel, across from A&Em Hotel). Open 24 hours!

This cafe is a unique experience for two reasons: you sit on little wooden stools watching the street, and the coffee is extremely, amazingly strong.

A cafe with little wooden chairs or stools where you sit on the street is Hanoi style, not Saigon style. But this is the new trend of cafes in Saigon. This cafe feels a little bit plain and old-fashioned, because most of the action is out on the street, and there's neither air conditioning nor wifi. It's great for watching people, both customers and the people walking by on the street. That's the new trend now in Saigon of these kinds of cafes, with small wooden stools, and no aircon or wifi. I guess it's retro. Maybe when this becomes the standard, air conditioned luxury cafes will be considered retro. Whatever. Welcome to Saigon.

You will see one interesting Vietnamese phenomenon at Cafe Vy. We Vietnamese people love to point out that in any other country, a cafe's seats would face toward the inside of the cafe, but in Vietnam, the cafe seats always face out onto the street. Much of the pleasure of going to a cafe is having a vantage point to watch the street and gossip with your friends about who and what you see.

Cafe Vy, unlike most Vietnamese cafes, has a list of different roasts of coffee you can try. They go up from #1 (cheapest) to #8 (most expensive). Most of them taste best iced and with milk (cafe sua da), so that's how I suggest you order them.

I like roast #4 (Huong Chon), but that's just me. "Huong Chon" means it smells like — but isn't — the famous "weasel coffee" you may have heard about.

99.9% of the "weasel coffee" you're sold or served in Vietnam has never been near any weasels. Other than the people selling it. (Thanks, I'll be here all week!) But Cafe Vy is honest. They don't claim it's actually weasel coffee, just that it tastes like it.

<u>Cafe Cheo Leo</u>
109/36 Nguyen Thien Thuat, Q3
Wifi password: caphevot
This is the oldest cafe in Saigon. I recommend it heartily. It's only open 6 AM until 6 PM, and it's closed on the 2nd and 15th of every month. The coffee is amazingly strong and cheap

MY SAIGON: THE LOCAL GUIDE TO HO CHI MINH CITY, VIETNAM

(under a dollar!), and the place oozes heritage and history. They play old (1970s-1980s) American, French, and Vietnamese pop music (with a weird occasional interspersing of "One More" by Ne Yo), there's no air conditioning, and people sit and chat all day.

It's really, truly Saigonese. Also, the neighborhood nearby, called *Ban Co*, is worth a look around. The street is famous for guitars (nowadays, mostly bought from China, so nothing special), but also has many interesting little restaurants and other cafes.

You can't access Cheo Leo directly by taxi, because the alley at 109 Nguyen Thien Thuat is usually blocked by parked motorcycles and street vendors. You have to go to the end of the alley and walk a bit into the alley.

Cafe Cheo Leo is house #36 on the alley that's at 109 Nguyen Thien Thuat. The easiest way to go there is to go to 130 Ly Thai To. Go near the big sushi and hotpot restaurant there, then look for the alley running perpendicular to Ly Thai To. The alley that Cheo Leo sits in runs from 130 Ly Thai To to

109 Nguyen Thien Thuat. Cheo Leo is much closer to the Ly Thai To end of the alley.

Got all that?! It's worth it, I promise!

Ban Ca Phe

387 Le Loi (up the sketchy stairwell), Q1

Wifi password: bancaphexinchao

Ban Ca Phe is a beautiful two-level cafe in an old apartment building, accessed through a rather unlikely-seeming alley. Ban is built to resemble a small library, with bookshelves and random vintage props lining the walls. It has tables, benches, and my favorite: sitting on pillows on the floor. It also has a balcony! It's a beautiful place to just chill — please don't be rowdy here, because it's a very calm and quiet place — and maybe use your laptop or read this book or whatever. The view onto Le Loi street is pretty nice too. The drinks are only mediocre.

Cong Cafe

26 Ly Tu Trong, Q1

(It's a chain, so there are also a few other locations in Saigon. The location on Mac Thi Buoi that was previously in this book has closed down.)

congcafe.com

This place advertises itself as a "hipster cafe." And in Vietnam, that's ok, even though I know that in the rest of the world, saying that you're a hipster automatically disqualifies you from being a hipster.

Cong Cafe is a bit of a nostalgia cafe, with combined overtones of nostalgia for Vietnam's hardline-communist days (the name "Cong" can mean something like "Communist"), as well as Saigon's pre-1975 pre-communist days. It's not really about politics though, but the service might remind you of a bread line in the Soviet Union. Somehow it's infamous for bad service. Also, nobody quite knows when it closes. One sign says midnight, another sign says 11 P.M., and once they kicked me and my laptop out at 9 P.M.

<u>Cafe Altec Lansing</u>
396 Nguyen Cong Tru, Q1

This is kind of an audio or listening bar cafe. They have a lot of vintage audio equipment in their stark white interior. It's hugely popular for Gen Z students and young tech/office workers group-working and hanging out.

Importantly, it's right next to the tourist areas of Pham Ngu Lao and central Q1, so you can probably even walk there from your hotel, but it's totally off the tourist track. It's a great way to get into "real" Saigonese coffee life without going geographically too far.

Drinks are good. It's open until 10:30PM. The baristas are deliberately chosen to be handsome (yes, many of the customers are women and gay men) and they do speak some English.

<u>Cafe 018</u>
18 Mac Tien Tich, Q 5, P 8

If you're from California, or even if you're not, you've seen "Vietnamese bikini cafes," right? Women in bikinis serve coffee. That's about it.

Cafe 018 is the closest you'll come to that in Vietnam. The young women working there wear tight, suggestive dresses and very short skirts, but not bikinis or lingerie. It might be fun for guys to visit — and I can guarantee that there will be no other foreigners there. Unless they've read this book.

It's on the ground floor of a run-down apartment building. Drinks aren't great. Don't expect anyone to speak English, but I think they'll be happy to serve you. It's just a fun experience, or can be.

You're expected to tip, probably about a level equal to your drink. So expect to spend 50K VND on your coffee and another 50K VND on the tip. Of course, they will ask you to tip more, but anything over 50K VND is totally optional.

Note that this is not a prostitution establishment, so please don't ask those kinds of questions. But sure, I'm sure the waitresses would love to have a "rich" boyfriend, so you're welcome to ask them out, along with the millions of "rich" Vietnamese guys who ask them out every day!

In addition to these places, you should look up locations of *Trung Nguyen Legend* on Google. It's a massive chain all around Saigon, and it's about the closest you can get these days to the traditional Vietnamese cafe experience: Vietnamese coffee drinks, table service, and food served. There used to be cafes like this on every corner ten years ago, but now they're being replaced by grab-and-go style cafes, or "third-wave" snobby places. Trung Nguyen is mostly keeping with the old style, although nowadays you do have to order and pay at the front counter, instead of sitting down and waving down a waiter.

They have a *pho kho Gia Lai* (dry pho: pho with the broth served separately, supposedly from the mountain town of Gia Lai) dish that is always a favorite. If you're staying on Ly Tu Trong Street, there's a Trung Nguyen Legend at 219 Ly Tu Trong.

Date street: Phan Xich Long

In the Phu Nhuan district, there's a street for going on dates. It's full of the usual complement of places needed for a date night in Saigon: trendy restaurant, cozy cafe, glitzy karaoke, and discreet love hotel. This street is basically one-stop shopping! And even if you're not particularly interested in the karaoke or the love hotel, you can enjoy the restaurants and cafes, as well as the atmosphere and people-watching.

Phan Xich Long is also near the river/canal walk I recommend on the parallel canal-side streets of Hoang Sa and Truong Sa. You can, as some Vietnamese couples do, combine your date with a walk along the canal.

I'm giving you a sampler of hangouts along this street, but there are dozens of places, so explore as you like, perhaps using my five recommendations as a starting point.

Squid noodles

A popular dinner place, and one of the few non-chain places here (young people on dates love chain places!) is Hu Tieu Muc Ong Gia Cali. That translates to Californian Old Grandpa's Squid Noodles. Great name for a restaurant, right? (In fact, it's such a great name for a restaurant that there are many fakes and derivatives of it around Saigon.)

It has a weird address: 001 Chung cu A3 Phan Xich Long. (Basically, it's at the ground floor of building A3 at the Phan Xich Long apartments.)

The menu has English. Your choices are squid noodle soup for 69K (yes, everyone in Vietnam gets the joke) or squid noodle soup with added shrimp for 79K. The shrimp don't do much for me, but you decide for yourself.

<u>Pasta Paradise</u>

This place, at 230 Phan Xich Long, is called Pasta Paradise! That's not a description I'm giving it, although it kind of is pasta paradise, at least by Vietnamese tastes. They do have difficult-to-find-in-Vietnam flavors such as pesto. But expect all your pasta dishes to be sugary, sugary sweet. Dishes cost around 100K; you're paying a premium for exotic foreign food. The key item you'll keep seeing on the menu is "mi y": that means Italian noodles. I'm not sure how Italian is, but it's noodles, and it's popular date food.

<u>Le Castella Cheesecake</u>

At 332 Phan Xich Long is a shop selling castella: a form of cheesecake popular in Taiwan and Japan. For about 120K-160K (depending on which flavor you choose), you get a cheesecake big enough for two people to share (once you go back to the love hotel, wink wink). Annoyingly, the wooden spoons they give you are totally flat. How can a spoon be flat? Ask them.

<u>Bun Cha Pho Co</u>

At 225 Phan Xich Long, there's one of Saigon's best regarded restaurants serving the northern specialty of bun cha: noodles with ground pork patty. We have to remember that in addition to Phan Xich Long being a date hangout, this neighborhood, Phu Nhuan, is also a northerner hangout. This is good bun cha for bun cha fans — not many of us Saigonese people like bun cha though.

<u>Gong Cha</u>

MY SAIGON: THE LOCAL GUIDE TO HO CHI MINH CITY, VIETNAM

At 181 Phan Xich Long is a tremendously popular and trendy bubble tea shop. To their credit, they're one of the few shops still using actual tea in their bubble tea. This is a small shop that often has a line out the door. For many of the customers, that's a feature, not a bug: it's time to spend with your date, or picking up other potential dates.

A note to LGBT friends: Phan Xich Long is very gay-friendly and all sorts of LGBT folks go on dates here. I see guys holding hands and walking arm-and-arm with each other here and nobody minds. (Visually obvious lesbians are rarer, but I'm no expert on the subject.) Just don't get into heavy PDA, because Vietnam doesn't like that, no matter what your orientation. That's what love hotels are for!

Oh, right: the love hotels. See all the places with usually three numbers posted outside? Those are all love hotels. If the sign says *can phong*, that means they have rooms available.

Actually, those love hotels can be a good option for budget lodging in Saigon. Most of their business is for an hour or two at a time, and they are happy to have any overnight business. Most of them post three prices outside: the price of the first hour, the price of the second hour, and the price of an overnight stay. So if the sign outside says "80 50 200," that means your first hour costs 80K VND, each additional hour costs 50K, and overnight costs 200K. If you don't mind staying in a windowless room in a seedy atmosphere (most of the "residents" are female sex workers holding "office hours"), these love hotels do have good locations and can be a lodging bargain.

Last thing, on a somewhat related topic: as much as I complain about foreigners thinking that every storefront in

Vietnam is a brothel, Linh Cherry Massage at 250 Phan Xich Long actually is a famous brothel. I guess in case date night doesn't go well! I wish places like that could somehow tell foreigners that they're not a massage shop, because I've heard of foreigners going there and being disappointed by the quality of massage. Going to that place for a massage is like going to Starbucks for a haircut.

Late-night Saigon

Saigon isn't quite The City That Never Sleeps. Most places do close around 9 or 10 PM. The law actually specifies that everything has to close by midnight — especially bars — but some businesses do get around it and are open late at night.

Most of what you'll find open late at night consists of food carts and temporary stands. A lot of it is near the backpacker area (Pham Ngu Lao) and in the popular night hangout area on Nguyen Trai Street near the New World Hotel. Those places are known for nightlife and for flexible police enforcement of the midnight closing time.

Aside from that, though, here are some well-known, established businesses where you can go for the hungries or the thirsties late at night, or maybe if you're just bored and want to see some people. All of these places are officially open 24 hours (except the banh mi place open 7 PM - 5 AM), although since this is Vietnam, I can't guarantee that all of them will always abide by that.

Pho Ong Cat Gia (201 Pham Ngu Lao, Q 1)

This is great pho. The only minor downsides to this place is that yes, most (but not all) of the customers are tourists, and yes, it's expensive by Vietnamese standards, at around 100K. I particularly like the chicken pho here.

This is right next to the Bui Vien Pham Ngu Lao drinking/party/backpacker street, so of course it gets a lot of the crowd from there.

Banh Mi Dem (65A Nguyen Thai Hoc, Q 1)
This longstanding banh mi stand is open only from 7 PM to 5 AM. There's only one auntie running the place. The most popular filling for the banh mi is siomai, usually called "shu mai" in English: pork meatballs.

Pho Ha (19 Hai Trieu, Q1)

This place is right next to Bitexco. It's mostly pho ga, chicken pho. There are competing shops around it, but Pho Ha is the only one that claims to be open 24 hours. In reality, it closes when the customer flow tapers off, usually around 2 AM — though it does stay open on 24 hours when the customers keep coming, which is usually only on weekend nights.

Din Ky (pronounced *yinky*) (137C Nguyễn Trãi, Q 1)

Din Ky is a big seafood restaurant for drunk people, gangsters, and prostitutes. That's a bit of a caricature, but it's not too far from the truth. They specialize in seafood and expensive meat dishes, especially game meat like crocodile and snake. Expect to spend at least 150K per person to eat here, and expect to see an "interesting" crowd. It's not dangerous or anything — it's in a very central area, and maybe non-Vietnamese people wouldn't even realize that most of these customers are involved in the Vietnamese criminal underworld. Just please don't stare at people and don't try to

MY SAIGON: THE LOCAL GUIDE TO HO CHI MINH CITY, VIETNAM

flirt with some tattooed guy's girlfriend or key his Bentley, ok? Din Ky claims to be open 24 hours but in reality usually closes around 3 AM. The food is good but not great. Be very careful ordering seafood here, because it's sold by weight, so if they quote you a price, it might be for only 100 grams, while what you're served is much more than that. If you run into trouble with the bill, just ask for help from the gangster at the next table.

<u>Bamos Cafe (69 Ngo Tất Tố, Q Bình Thạnh)</u>

Bamos is a new and amazingly nice 24-hour place in an old big French concrete house. It's usually quiet and peaceful and full of studying students and working coders. It's very much a laptop place. Note it's a bit difficult to find from the street, as it's inside a small courtyard off the street. You'll find it. Just go inside the courtyard and you'll see it. If you see me working there, say hi. Actually, please don't. I'm shy IRL.

ELLY THUY NGUYEN

Cafe Vy (277E Le Thanh Ton, Q 1)

Cafe Vy is a classic longtime 24-hour street hangout spot on the street near Ben Thanh Market, and in fact across the street from the A & Em hotel I usually recommend to visitors. There's great, strong coffee, rows of small seats facing the street, and always a crowd of people watching street goings-on, even at very odd hours. (Fun fact: some of those people at Cafe Vy are gangsters watching mafia-controlled business activity. It's a great vantage point!) Unfortunately there are many smokers here, but it's outdoors (under a roof), so the wind blows away some but not all of the smoke. Also, this place isn't really set up for working on a laptop, though I've done it.

Three O'Clock Coffee (462 Nguyen Thi Minh Khai, Q 3)

Three O'Clock is a huge former indoor parking garage that's been converted into a 24-hour cafe. The crowd here is pretty loud and pretty rough. I wouldn't come here expecting to work quietly on a laptop, but it's a good place to see average twentysomething Saigonese culture. (I think the Bamos crowd is more like elite students and the Cafe Vy crowd is kind of rich.) Unfortunately, the coffee here is awful — I don't think it's even coffee — so just order a tea or a sugary "juice" drink or something.

Note: The famous old Caphe Vot at 330 Phan Dinh Phung in Phu Nhuan was open for 24 hours for many years, but now

MY SAIGON: THE LOCAL GUIDE TO HO CHI MINH CITY, VIETNAM

closes at 9 PM — in case you see it recommended elsewhere as a 24 hour place.

ELLY THUY NGUYEN

Ben Thanh Market, local style

I've told you not to shop at Ben Thanh Market. That advice still stands. I've never heard of any Vietnamese people shopping at Ben Thanh Market in probably the past decade. It's an awful place and a big tourist trap.

However, there is some decent food from the food stands inside Ben Thanh Market — I mean the stands that serve food to eat right away, *not* the awful places that sell inedible packaged food and coffee and the like.

Also, in addition to the food inside Ben Thanh, there are some interesting places on the streets immediately outside Ben Thanh.

As you might expect, the food stands at Ben Thanh that are aggressively trying to pull you in to sit down and waving menus in your face are not the good ones. The good ones have lots of Vietnamese customers already and don't care about attracting tourists.

One particularly good stall is called Be Che. Literally, the name means *Dessert Baby*, and this place sells traditional Vietnamese desserts, *che*. They have different sweet substances in those cups and containers — you can just ask them to mix up whatever you want, or pick something from their simple English menu. It's sugary but delicious, and isn't that what dessert should always be?

The most famous food inside Ben Thanh Market is banh beo. It's white round rice cakes. The stall selling it is off to the side, and just says *Banh Beo Hue 25,000*. Hold up a finger and you'll get a plate of banh beo. I think in English they're called *Hue rice cakes* or something like that.

For some reason, banh beo is a dish popular almost exclusively with women. The crowd eating at this shop is always almost entirely groups of office women. So if you're looking for a Vietnamese girlfriend — I don't know, but I'm just giving you some intel. (By the way, *banh beo* is also Vietnamese slang for a shallow, materialistic woman, probably because like those rice cakes, she is slim, white-skinned, and flavorless.)

Also good is stall 1006, called Thanh Tri, selling banh cuon (rice-flour rolls, I think sometimes called spring rolls in English, but these are served hot). Look for the yellow signs saying *Banh Cuon Thanh Tri*. Their English menu calls those rolls *ravioli* which is I guess close enough, but there's no cheese inside, just meat and vegetables.

MY SAIGON: THE LOCAL GUIDE TO HO CHI MINH CITY, VIETNAM

Now, on the streets outside? At 6 Nguyen An Ninh, there's an ancient barber shop that's been around for decades but has no name and no Google Maps listing. Let's just say that if you're not old enough to collect US Social Security, you're guaranteed to be the youngest customer there. It's a cool place to view for the atmosphere. I honestly have not gone for a haircut here, but I'm sure I have some uncles who are regular customers.

At 35 Phan Chu Trinh, there's a hipster "third wave" cafe called Soo Kafe. It's almost totally hidden, and you have to go upstairs after finding the nearly unmarked door. True hipster, right?

At the intersection of Phan Chu Trinh and Le Thanh Ton (in front of 49 Phan Chu Trinh), there's a lady with a cart selling *nuoc mia*: fresh-squeezed sugarcane juice. She's been there for decades and has enough regular customers so as not to care about attracting tourists. One glass costs 30K.

At 140 Le Thanh Ton is Thanh Binh, a longstanding (since the 1960s) crab noodle soup restaurant in Saigon. It's good stuff, though expensive for Vietnamese standards, like 100K range. Please avoid the fake down the street that has the English-language sign *crab noodle soup*. That one is fake and a tourist trap. The real crab noodle soup place is at 140 Le Thanh Ton and the sign only says

Quan An Thanh Binh. See, the good places don't need to chase after foreigners' business.

At 104 Le Thanh Ton, there's Vit Van, a longstanding (among Vietnamese customers!) shop selling really good takeout *goi vit* and *goi ga*: duck salad and chicken salad, respectively. These aren't "salad" like the American mayonnaise style salad. They're just chunks of that meat tossed usually with green papaya and vegetables. One box might cost around 200K and is meant to share, but I won't tell if you eat it yourself. They also sell whole and half roast duck and roast chicken. Yum. Not cheap though.

At 15 Nguyen Trung Truc is Xoi Ga Number One. This place famously specializes in sticky rice with chicken, *xoi ga*, for an entirely local crowd. A plate of *xoi ga* costs 30K and they're a bit curt with foreigners because they're tired of being asked if they serve pho. No, there's no pho.

At 157 Le Thanh Ton there's the weirdly named Cheese Coffee. This place is so high-falutin' that the entrance is difficult to find. It's the small yellow door off to the side, not the big door. And the signs only say *Cheese XX Marche*. I think foreigners don't even know this is a cafe.

This — and only this — branch of Cheese Coffee is a super-elite see-and-be-seen Vietnamese hangout.

MY SAIGON: THE LOCAL GUIDE TO HO CHI MINH CITY, VIETNAM

There are always celebrities doing photoshoots here. Everyone here has money or fame or something like that. Except for me, because I also like to sit here for the people-watching.

Walking Ban Co Market

Didn't I just tell you to avoid traditional Vietnamese markets?

Look, I can explain.

Ban Co isn't really a market. It's not a roofed place with people ripping you off. It's a collection of small streets in Q 3 that are informally known as a market, *cho ban co*, but are really more like a neighborhood. *Ban co* means *chessboard*, and this is a neighborhood of small gridded streets and alleys, like a chessboard.

This is real, old-timey Saigon, with very few foreigners. And there are cafes and food shops to stop along here, not just raw meat and ripoff vendors.

Maybe a good starting point (or ending point) for your Ban Co explorations is Cafe Cheo Leo. This is the oldest cafe in Saigon. It's at 139/36 Nguyen Thien Thuat. That's house #36 on Alley 139 for Nguyen Thien Thuat. Like most of Ban co, the alley is too small for cars. But the easiest way to get to Cafe Cheo Leo is to start at the Spice World Hotpot restaurant at 120 Ly Thai To. A car can drop you off there, and then Cheo Leo is just around the corner. It's a lovely place, open only 6 AM to 6 PM, with three grandmas serving coffee to a crowd of customers who have been coming there for decades.

You can also have much more modern coffee just down the alley at Cafe Muoi. That's salt coffee. Their specialty is salty cream coffee, which is a new trend, and which I promise is good. They're at 111 Nguyen Thien Thuat in a space that is sort of a big metal box, not really a building.

Just around the corner from Cheo Leo, at 718 Nguyen Dinh Chieu, there's a very classic and very historic *che* (Vietnamese dessert) shop called Hien Khanh. I'm sure most foreigners don't even know this is a dessert shop. It looks kind of dark and mysterious from the outside. They do have a basic English menu, they do their best to accommodate foreigners. They specialize in traditional Cantone— I mean Vietnamese desserts such as lychee jelly and sweet red bean soup for around 25K each. Note that to add to the mystery, Hien Khanh is closed from noon to 2:30 PM. Owners gotta eat! (Actually, they say it's too hot to operate a dessert shop midday.)

There's absolutely classic VFC, Vietnamese fried chicken, at 172 Nguyen Thien Thuat. The place is called Hoang Ky. They do have an English menu. I recommend *ga chien nuoc mam*, chicken fried with fish sauce. The key ingredient is the fried onions. This is delicious stuff, and the old folks have been eating their VFC at Hoang Ky since the 1980s.

There's an old-school *mi gia*, Cantonese noodle shop, called Ong Map (*Fat Grandpa*) at 175/7 Nguyen Thien Thuat. They have dimsum classics like *ha cao* (hargao) and *xiu mai* (siomai), in addition to the usual *mi hai san* (seafood noodle soup). This place is old and great.

You can also eat some generally inferior (really) Cantonese food at Hua Wu Lou at 27C Ban Co Street (there's an actual street called Ban Co, which comprises only part of the neighborhood called Ban Co). Hua Wu Lou is not historic and it's a mediocre dimsum place that has one standout dish: the last item on the menu, the cheese crab shell. It's crab and cheese baked inside a crab shell, and it's absolutely delicious. Most people go there just for this dish actually. The other stuff — the dimsum — isn't very good, and the service is surly.

Around Ban Co, if it's before 1 PM, you should also visit Banh Mi Chao Bue Due Co Le — that's already recommended in the "hot plate breakfast" section of this book. In the alley of 213 Nguyen Thien Thuat, there's an apartment building, and if you look around (or use Google Maps set for Banh Mi Chao Bue Due Co Le), you'll see Co Le set up at her colorful cart. There's a photo of her in the hot plate breakfast section of this book. Generally you can wander those alleys around the apartment building — I'm sorry, but there is no real address to give you there, because people just call it *chung cu Nguyen Thien Thuat*, *the apartment buildings on Nguyen Thien Thuat*.

The closest thing to an actual wet market at Ban Co happens in the mornings (6 AM - 11 AM) around 533 Nguyen Dinh Chieu, where there's a column saying *Cho Ban Co*. Not really much there for someone who's not shopping for raw meat or fish or something, but you can take a look.

There is currently (2024) a proposal to make Ban Co the new backpacker district (like Pham Ngu Lao), and another proposal to make it a "nightlife district," whatever the heck that means. Let Ban Co be Ban Co, I say, but I'm kind of a traditionalist (in some ways!).

Cat cafe

Maybe you've heard of cat cafes. They're a thing now in many places in the world. You have coffee and play with some resident cats. Thanks to the lack of stringent health regulations here in Vietnam, we've had cat cafes much longer than almost any other country.

Please note that the previously most famous cat cafe in Saigon, Ailu / Tokyo Cat Cafe, closed down in September 2019 during Covid.

Instead of Ailu, there's Catfe at 119 Nguyen Thi Minh Khai. It's three stories of playing-with-cats fun! Thanks to cat cafes hitting the mainstream, Catfe is right in the city center — you used to have to hit Saigon's outer reaches to visit a cat cafe. It's a popular place to go mostly for college-aged Saigonese people.

You are likely to see a friendly group of teen and twentysomething Saigonese couples playing with and especially photographing cats. They might be eager to speak some English with you! Also, foreign cat lovers often come to see cats. You're unlikely to see Vietnamese people above about age thirty, perhaps because playing with cats is considered childish, or perhaps because the love of cats as pets is a novelty still in Vietnam.

ELLY THUY NGUYEN

Five floors of hipsters for a rainy day

Central Saigon has many now-crumbling pre-1975-vintage apartment buildings. There's a trend of converting those buildings into hipsters' hangouts. And the currently most prominent example of an old apartment building turned into a mall of hipstering is at 14 Ton That Dam, next to the (unmarked) National Bank of Vietnam.

14 Ton That Dam has hip cafes, small restaurants, clothing shops, and "vintage" type stuff. Hipsterdom. The nice thing about the building is that you are in one building, so it's a perfect activity on a rainy day – allowing you to see many things without needing to go out in the rain.

Look carefully for 14 Ton That Dam, because it's marked as sort of an alley entrance, an old sign that currently says "MTV." Go into the alley, and see the old concrete stairs flaring upward on your right side. Yes, those concrete stairs, the really old-looking ones. When the building was first being hipsterized, the stairway was unmarked, but now it's been marked, mostly in English, pointing your way up, up, up to five floors of hipsterdom.

The elevator has been removed from the building, leaving an open elevator shaft, and, more importantly, limiting the upper floors to those who have decent cardiovascular endurance (or who stopped for coffee and sweets on the way up). The stairs can be slippery and probably don't meet even Vietnamese safety standards. And when it rains, there are phantom water droplets flying all over the building. So don't expect anything too pretty. But expect something pretty cool.

Perhaps the most well known cafe at this building is Cafe Banksy, dedicated to the British street artist Banksy. There may also be a pun in play – although I'm not sure whether the cafe is aware of it – because the cafe looks out onto the National Bank of Vietnam.

Possibly the hippest, because the most difficult to access (top floor) cafe here is Mockingbird Cafe, yes, on the very top floor. They have a concrete balcony overlooking the street below where it's kind of magical to sit in the evenings.

Q: How many hipsters does it take to change a light bulb?
A: It's a really obscure number; you wouldn't know it.

A few Facebook links:
https://www.facebook.com/BanksyCafe
https://www.facebook.com/mockingbirdcoffee
https://www.facebook.com/thingscafe
https://www.facebook.com/TheOtherPersonCafe

There are also clusters of old-apartment-building cafes at 26 Ly Tu Trong, 9 Thai Van Lung, 42 Nguyen Hue, and 158D Pasteur, all in Quan 1.

Four ultra-hipster cafes

Yo, I heard you like hipsters? Or maybe you like laughing at hipsters. Or maybe you just want to show off your magnificent ironic mustache.

Whatever. I've got you covered. Here are four cafes you can visit and meet all the right people. Or all the wrong people.

All these places are in Q1. It's an obscure quan; you've never heard of it.

<u>Hoang Thi</u>

14 Ton That Dam (Second floor for Americans, first floor for the rest of the world. No, there aren't separate entrances. I mean Americans start counting floor numbers at the ground floor. You know what I mean.) Turn left from the stairwell.

Hoang Thi is hipster overload. If Vietnamese people could grow ironic mustaches, every single one of the patrons here would have one. Or two even.

The darkened space is full of spinning disco balls and flashing multicolored lights. There is tons of random furniture, including a very comfy soft chair on the balcony looking outside. And the wifi password is **quyxuonghamiengra** which in Vietnamese means... *kneel down and open wide*. I'm not making this up.

During the day, there are indie bands practicing here. At night, it can get pretty crowded, as there aren't that many actual seats.

The drinks are terrible, because of course they are. The cafe sua da tastes like sugar milk. They do serve alcohol if you want to drown your sorrows. Coffee drinks are around 60K VND and alcoholic drinks are around 150K VND.

The employees are infamous for having a "too cool for you" attitude. I saw some Tripadvisor reviews claiming that the employees are "racist" or "don't like foreigners." Nope, they're rude to us Vietnamese people too, so don't worry. We're all equal here. But we just keep coming back. What was that about kneeling down and opening wide?

Big minus: Smoking. And, of course, the biggest smokers are the employees. Because of course.

Shin Heritage

13 Nguyen Thiep

This is kind of the opposite end of the hipster spectrum from Hoang Thi.

The drinks here are amazingly good, and at 100K a pop, they should be. The space is serene and the service is impeccable. Sometimes it does get completely full, and when there are no more seats, well, there are no more seats.

They have all the pourover glassware equipment that looks like something from Breaking Bad. They have the necessary sign that says "specialty coffee." And so on.

This is where Saigon's celebrities and nouveau riche drink coffee. A lot of the customers get dropped off in Bentleys or whatever else those monstrous cars are. Today I was there and saw three Porsches in a row pull up and block the street while waiting for a cup of takeout coffee. Because in Communism, everyone is equal. Oops, I didn't just say that.

There are some really nice seats next to the bay window where you can look out onto the world while drinking your

MY SAIGON: THE LOCAL GUIDE TO HO CHI MINH CITY, VIETNAM

100K vnd cup of coffee! For some reason, many newlywed couples take photos outside this cafe.

Shin Heritage started as a Japanese-owned place just called Shin, but now it's called Shin Heritage and it's been acquired by a Vietnamese dude who owns a lot of hipster establishments around Saigon, most with *Heritage* in the name — most of which fail, actually. I don't know where he gets his money, but I don't ask.

This place is right next to the Nguyen Hue walking area, so it can be fun to combine with a Nguyen Hue adventure. Just remember that Shin closes at 6:30 PM, because hipsters have places to be.

<u>The Workshop</u>
27 Ngo Duc Ke

We get it. We totally get it. You're third-wave, specialty coffee. You're in an industrial loft. You're up four flights of stairs and there's no elevator. Your seats are tiny, hard wooden stools.

Congratulations: you've checked all the boxes. You are indeed a hipster cafe. You even serve flat whites, which are lattes for hipsters and Australians. (Thanks, I'll be here all week.)

The reward for climbing those stairs is a pretty great view from an old apartment loft out onto central Saigon. The non-reward is that they either don't run the air conditioning or it's underpowered, because this place always seems uncomfortably too hot. Maybe sweating is hip.

They also have food. It's not cheap. But then neither is art school.

<u>Lacaph Experience</u>

220 Nguyen Cong Tru (go in the unmarked stairwell on the ground floor, because of course, and climb up the stairs to the glass patio door)

I joke, but the coffee at Korean-owned Lacaph is amazing. They have creative drinks that actually work, like salted coffee, pina colada coffee (with coconut milk), and egg coffee that doesn't taste like eggs. The drinks taste spectacular.

They also have seminars and classes and, yes, coffee experiences that you can book online but are much cheaper if you book them at the actual location.

Lots of foreign tourists come here, and it's also a gathering spot (Vietnamese language lesson: *hoi quan*) for everyone in Saigon who calls themselves "a creative" or claims to work in design, digital marketing, digital presence, or synergy channels. Ok, I made up that last one.

There's a weird setup where there's a cashier sitting all by herself in the empty lobby. I don't know if she gets bored there, because this place doesn't have many customers. But the drinks really are amazing.

Four Saigon street food streets

Everybody loves the street food. And it's everywhere around us in Saigon. Some twenty years ago, Ben Thanh Market was the place for street food in Saigon. Nowadays, Ben Thanh is still around, but it's become mostly a tourist trap. Sure, you can go there, but the food isn't great, and for anything other than food, it's extremely overpriced and of extremely poor quality. That and it's just a hassle to deal with the aggressive vendors.

Instead, let me introduce you to some other places in Saigon where you can experience a lot of street food stalls clustered together. These are definitely not the only places in Saigon to find street food! They're just places with high concentrations of it.

Ho Thi Ky Street, Q10

Q10 sounds daunting, but this isn't far from the center. Q10 is just outside Q3 actually.

Ho Thi Ky is officially a flower market. If you're into flowers, well, Ho Thi Ky is your uncle. But nowadays, the food section at Ho Thi Ky has become a bigger deal than the flower section.

Ho Thi Ky is famous for being cheap, and on Vietnamese social media, there's the "Ho Thi Ky 100K challenge": showing off how much amazing food you can buy for 100K VND (about $4) at Ho Thi Ky.

The downside to Ho Thi Ky is the vendors don't speak English. But what is there to talk about? The food is out on display, the price is usually posted, so pay your money and get your noodles. While I can't vouch for every vendor here treating you well (I mean, people are people), this doesn't strike me as a place where foreigners would be cheated or overcharged. I think if anything, you'll be welcomed as a novelty, because Ho Thi Ky is still almost an entirely Vietnamese crowd.

Unlike the crowd though, the food at Ho Thi Ky is not entirely Vietnamese. Believe it or not, we Vietnamese people also like to eat exotic foreign food, and one thing Ho Thi Ky is famous for is foreign (that is, non-Vietnamese) food at low prices. Usually foreign food in Vietnam is priced at a premium, but not so at Ho Thi Ky.

Ho Thi Ky is sometimes colloquially called "Cambodian Market" by Saigonese people, as in the past most of the vendors there were from Cambodia. That's not true anymore — though there are a few Cambodian grilled beef stalls — though that name still sort of persists.

Standout dishes and stall numbers at Ho Thi Ky: Beef spring rolls at 57/23B, pad thai at 87/24, lamb rice at 105B

MY SAIGON: THE LOCAL GUIDE TO HO CHI MINH CITY, VIETNAM

(and Korean fried chicken directly across from it), and egg and cheese dumplings at 438/44.

There's also a ton of seafood, especially shrimp, crabs, and oysters.

Of course vendors come and go, so don't be too shocked if these dishes aren't at these stall numbers anymore. Just dive in and eat. That's what you're there for.

<u>Ha Ton Quyen Street, Q11</u>

This street in Q11 (which is right next to Q5) specializes in just one dish: sui cao, soup dumplings. These are Cantonese-style dumplings, usually served in noodle soup, or fried and served standalone.

There are about ten restaurants and street stalls all selling the same dish. Sorry, not much variety. But this place is absolutely hopping, especially around 10PM until midnight.

English? No, sorry. Cantonese? Haiya, haiya!

I suggest the restaurant Ngoc Y, 187 Ha Ton Quyen. And if you don't want to go all the way to Q11, Ngoc Y delivers on Grab Food. Ask me how I know!

<u>Ton That Dam Street, Q1</u>

Or as I like to call it, Ton That Dyaaamn!

Yes, it's that good. And it's conveniently located right in the middle of Q1, close to the hipster apartment/cafe building at 14 Ton That Dam.

There are small food stalls selling everything, and also some full-scale restaurants. My favorite restaurant is Mi Quang Anh Em at 74 Ton That Dam. Mi Quang is a dish of noodles "with everything," basically, and it is much better than pho, trust me. You can ask for Mi Quang Dac Biet, which is "the special" and costs about 80K VND, and your Mi Quang will have really everything in it. (And Anh Em in the name? You should recognize that by now: those are the two main pronouns in Vietnamese, older bother and younger sibling.)

You can ask for Grab or taxi to take you to 74 Ton That Dam and they won't be able to get all the way to the restaurant, but they'll have to stop basically where the pedestrian area begins, and you'll have to suffer through all the delicious sights and smells as you try to make your way uninterrupted from your taxi to whatever restaurant you're going to! Or be like me and make some eating stops along the way. Quite a few of them, in fact.

<u>Nguyen Thuong Hien Street, Q3</u>

The good thing about Nguyen Thuong Hien is that it's very centrally located in Q3. The bad thing about it is that while it's a street food street, it's set up for motorcycles, not for pedestrians, so there are motorcycles always running around between the stalls and it's a bit scary to be walking there. Sorry.

Nguyen Thuong Hien sells tons of stuff, but it's most famous for two things: gyros (yes, gyros, which in Vietnam we call "Turkish bread," *banh mi tho ni ky*), and banh trang tron (especially at 38 Nguyen Thuong Hien), which is a dried noodle salad street snack that's also sold at Turtle Lake (also covered in this book).

Very near Nguyen Thuong Hien, on the cross street Vo Van Tan, is Yen Huong Giang, which is arguably the best bun bo hue (cinnamon beef noodle soup) in Saigon, at 323 Vo Van Tan, Q3. Also nearby is a famous place selling chuoi nep nuong, which is a grilled banana and rice dessert, at 378 Vo Van Tan. So much to eat, so little calorie budget!

Saigon screams for ice cream

Every foreign visitor "knows" that in Saigon, we eat pho 99% of the time, and the other 1% of the time, we're barbecuing your dog. But did you know — for real now — that Saigonese people absolutely love ice cream?

Ice cream is huge in Saigon, and certainly a lot more popular than pho. It may be even more popular than barbecuing your dog! When we go to hang out with our friends, if we're not drinking coffee, then most likely we're eating ice cream.

The word for ice cream is *kem*. It's the Vietnamization of the word *cream*. There's also *kem ý*, where *ý* is the Vietnamization of *Italy*. And lastly, there's a new trend of referring to ice cream as *ca rem* which is — let me gather my notes here — a Vietnamization of the Thai-ization of the word *ice cream*. *Ca rem* is supposedly Thailand style ice cream.

(Language note: When the letter e is just a plain e, *kem* means ice cream. When the e has an accent-mark thingie over it, it means *failed* or *inadequate*. Don't worry: I've already taken the lead on making the most of this pun when posting negative online reviews of ice cream shops.)

Now you know what those street vendors advertising *kem* are selling. I think they really miss out on a business opportunity by not having an English translation, or at least a picture of an ice cream cone, because they're usually selling their ice cream out of a closed cooler, and foreigners will have no idea what's on offer.

ELLY THUY NGUYEN

Where to eat ice cream in Saigon? Twenty years ago, there would've been one obvious answer: Bach Dang Ice Cream at 26 Le Loi, just down the street from Ben Thanh Market.

Twenty years ago, not only was Ben Thanh a good place to go eat, but Bach Dang (pronounced *bat dang*) had pretty much a monopoly on the ice cream business in central Saigon, and they occupied an entire multi-story building. It was crowded with families (including Little Elly and family) every weekend.

Now, Bach Dang is a relic. It occupies a small shop space on the ground-floor corner of the building at 26 Le Loi where it once ruled over the whole building. It's no longer an air-conditioned indoor place, but an open-air coffee place. It's very expensive, and the ice cream tastes like it's from a convenience store. The whole situation is just too sad to think about, so let's move on to what ice cream places are actually good now:

For expensive old-school Saigonese ice cream with a view, I recommend one of the outlets of Brodard anywhere in central Saigon, but especially the one at 133 Dong Khoi. It is smack in the center of the city, near Nguyen Hue walking street, it has a wonderful people-watching view, it's a historical-looking (even if not actually old) building and shop, it's clean, they speak English, and the ice cream is pretty good.

Downside? You'll pay around 200K VND for your ice cream. That's not a misprint. Yes, it's expensive. (And water isn't free! Add another 50K or so.) When we Vietnamese people go to Brodard, we make it worth it, by basically spending all afternoon or evening hanging out there with our 200K VND ice cream.

MY SAIGON: THE LOCAL GUIDE TO HO CHI MINH CITY, VIETNAM

Do you want to have ice cream in the same Nguyen Hue walking street area, but with much more reasonable prices and a much younger crowd? Check out Snowee at 39 Nguyen Hue. It's technically gelato, not ice cream. It overlooks the walking street. It does tend to be crowded, often with screaming teenagers. I guess I'm getting old.

By the way, on the Nguyen Hue walking street itself, you'll see some street vendors with *kem*. The new trend is "kem khoi Han Quoc," which means "Korean smoke ice cream." Fortunately, this has nothing to do with cigarettes, but just that the ice cream has "smoke" vapors, like dry ice vapors, coming from it. I don't think it's a big deal, but the teenagers love it. I really am getting old.

There's some great local people and street watching at an ice cream shop called Bud's on Phan Xich Long (a famous walking / hangout street) in Quan Phu Nhuan. Bud's is apparently a US chain that nobody in the US has ever heard of. They do pretty good business in Saigon. But the main treat here is being able to watch not just people inside the shop, but also out on the street on Phan Xich Long — and you are very likely to be the only foreigner. The actual address is 32 Hoa Dao, Q Phu Nhuan. It's at the intersection of Phan Xich Long and Hoa Dao. (Bonus: Remember Luu Gia, the egg coffee place I recommended? It's about a three-minute walk from Bud's, just on the other side of Phan Xich Long. Prepare your pancreas.)

Near the Pham Ngu Lao cesspoo— I mean backpacker district, there's Roseice at 4 Tran Hung Dao. Vietnam loves gendering all kinds of places, and this is an ice cream place meant for women. It's gelato. It has an Insta-friendly pink interior.

For serious ice cream eating and a pretty good value, go to I Love Kem 260 Le Hong Phong in Quan 5. This is "self serve" ice cream: get whatever you want, and pay by weight at the end. The location itself isn't inspiring, and the neighborhood is kind of drab, but if it's large amounts of reasonably priced ice cream that you're after, this is your place.

Final note: You may see other sources sending you to an ice cream place called Fanny. It's closed down. It was huge a few years ago, but no more. Maybe people found out what that word means in English. I don't know.

MY SAIGON: THE LOCAL GUIDE TO HO CHI MINH CITY, VIETNAM

Chinatown alley for your Insta

Hao Si Phuong is a residential alley in Saigon's Quan 5 ("Chinatown") that used to be sort of forgotten, but now is huge. Huge, I tell you! All thanks to Instagram and music videos and other outlets.

It's a hundred-year-old residential alley full of colorful buildings, shophouses, and lanterns, a bit like Hoi An I guess. It's a nice way to see a picturesque, idealized version of Saigon life back in the day.

It is now *the* hot place to make your music video or your model photoshoot. Actually, most Saigonese people don't even know where it is, just that it's that place that always shows up in ads and music videos. Some people actually think it's a movie set, not a real place, because it looks so overwhelmingly "vintage" that it can't be real.

If you Google "Hao Si Phuong," you'll find approximately nine gazillion photos of it.

It's at 206 Tran Hung Dao, Quan 5, Phuong 11, near the traditional neighborhood temple where I sent you. Just go inside the gate at 206 Tran Hung Dao. It should have the words "Hao Si Phuong" written above it.

Note that it's a real place where real people live. They're used to having tourists and moviemakers coming through, but just be aware they're not paid actors, just people, generally older people, trying to live their lives, so try to be polite and not make too much noise.

MY SAIGON: THE LOCAL GUIDE TO HO CHI MINH CITY, VIETNAM

There are usually coffee and food vendors hanging around, and you can be a good visitor by buying from them plentifully. Coffee costs around 20,000 VND and a meal around 30,000 VND. Just like in the old days!

ELLY THUY NGUYEN

Egg coffee and a river walk

Thanks to some food-oriented TV shows, nowadays many tourists want to try Hanoi's egg coffee.

Egg coffee was invented out of necessity in North Vietnam. The government collectivized big farms, and that meant there was no more milk available. But people still kept chickens at home — so even if they didn't have milk, they did have eggs, and they started thinking up ways to substitute eggs for milk.

Egg coffee used to be available in only one place in Saigon, on a stretch of Hoa Cuc street in Phu Nhuan, near Phan Xich Long street. Nowadays, thanks to the tourists asking for egg coffee, it's available in many places in Saigon, including Lacaph and Shin cafes above.

But you can still try Saigon's original egg coffee: Cafe Luu Gia, 8 Hoa Cuc. See http://luugiacafe.com/ Outside of Hoa Cuc Street, when this book first came out, you'd really have to fly to Hanoi to drink egg coffee. Nowadays, largely thanks to tourists, there's egg coffee all over Saigon.

Make sure you're going to the real Cafe Luu Gia; there are copies of it all around Hoa Cuc Street. The shop called Carina next door to the real one is an exact copy, but still a copy. (Confession: Carina is such a good copy that I mistakenly went in once. The egg coffee isn't bad actually, but as a matter of principle, I don't patronize copies.)

Egg coffee isn't really popular among Saigonese people. We consider it a novelty drink to try once. Most of the demand is from tourists.

Near Cafe Luu Gia is a nice and very undiscovered-by-tourists area for a riverside walk in urban Saigon. There's an inlet of the Saigon River winding around through the area intersecting Q 3, Q 1, and Q Phu Nhuan. The two streets – on the two sides of the "river" – are named Hoang Sa and Truong Sa, which are the two groups of Vietnamese islands that China is attempting to seize.

Hoang Sa and Truong Sa, the streets, have, unusually for Saigon, foot paths that are great for a leisurely walk or even a jog along the river. If you want a starting point, you may want to go to Cafe Cay Cot Dien at 627 Hoang Sa, but anywhere in that neighborhood is fine. I don't advise going there after dark – it's not dangerous, but there are many riverside bars, and there's a risk of rowdy drunk people acting like rowdy drunk people.

No turtles, no lake, but a great evening hangout

On Pham Ngoc Thach street, at its intersection with Vo Van Tan street, in the very center of Q1, very close to the famous church and Diamond Plaza, there is a small urban pond called Turtle Lake in English, or Ho Con Rua (same meaning) in Vietnamese. The official, post-1975 name of the street circling the lake is Cong Truong Quoc Te ("international circle"), but nobody calls it that.

There's a small pond, a sitting area with benches, and a concrete stairway up to a concrete patio or sitting and viewing area up above the pond. As an attraction in itself, it's nothing special. But in the evenings, it's a popular gathering place for people, especially college-age people, usually chatting and eating snacks and street food. It's almost... magical... with the evening air, the pond in the middle of Saigon, and the smell of street food cooking. Sorry for being sentimental! Anyway, despite its proximity to tourist attractions, I've never seen any foreigners hanging out there.

The street food sold there is a great selection, and it may be the best place to get Vietnamese street food in Q1. The perennial favorite street food of Vietnamese college students is banh trang tron, which is kind of a dry noodle salad. Another popular choice is xoi bap, sticky rice balls fried with corn. And my personal favorite is banh trang nuong, sometimes called "Vietnamese pizza," but which I consider more akin to a taco – it has exactly the same ingredients as banh trang tron (that noodle salad), but instead of the dough being made into dried noodles and mixed up, the dough is baked into a cake (like a tortilla) and the toppings are put on top of it. The lady usually selling banh trang nuong has a sign that says NUONG in big letters, and then "banh trang" in smaller letters – so know what you're looking for.

Another dish, often sold alongside banh trang nuong, is banh trung. Banh means cake and trung means egg. They're kind of like egg souffles, made in a tiny saucepan held over an open flame. And now my mouth is watering.

One portion of banh trang tron or banh trang nuong or banh trung should cost you no more than 20,000 VND. I don't think the vendors speak any English, but how hard can it be to point and pay? The corn rice balls (xoi bap) usually go for around 8,000 VND each. There are also drinks and coffee, costing around 15,000 VND each.

And every business establishment on the street circling the pond is a cafe, so if you get tired of sitting outside, you can always move inside to a cafe. It's a good selection of Saigon cafes, and you may even find a favorite hangout for yourself – with a view on Turtle Lake.

I don't recommend staying at Turtle Lake later than 10 PM. At 10 PM, the surrounding cafes close, and the crowd at the pond becomes kind of rough. It's not a warzone or anything, but I'm not comfortable staying there after 10 PM, and you might not be either.

MY SAIGON: THE LOCAL GUIDE TO HO CHI MINH CITY, VIETNAM

A walk in the park

Want a respite from motorcycles? Want to walk without fear of getting run over? Want to see greenery, and even birds? Come to Tao Dan Park! It's right in the center of Saigon, and is open 5 AM to 10 PM every day. The best time to go is in the early morning, and I don't advise going after sunset.

Tao Dan was originally built by the French in 1869, and called *Jardin de la Ville*, which of course just means *City Garden*. That makes it only eleven years newer than New York City's Central Park! In addition to a park, the French built a school, a library, and other public facilities there. (By the way, contrary to today's Vietnamese government propaganda, most Saigonese people are pretty fond of our former French overlords. I'm no apologist for colonialism, but I'm just reporting the facts!)

Tao Dan park adjoins the South Vietnam Presidential Palace (now known as the Reunification Palace) for a very specific reason: it was previously part of the same complex. That palace was originally the palace of the French governor of Saigon, and the garden (open to the public) adjoined the palace.

The park doesn't have an address, but you can ask for "Cong Vien Tao Dan" or enter that into your Grab app. *Cong vien* just means *park*. Tao Dan Park It's bordered by Nguyen Thi Minh Khai, Truong Dinh, and Cach Mang Thang 8 ("CMT8") streets. Everybody knows where it is. It's like asking for Central Park in New York City.

One of the most notable things at Tao Dan is a temple to the Hung Vuong kings. You can look around inside. There are also ponds, fountains, statues, and even a (gross, crowded, dirty, not recommended) public swimming pool. There are also people playing hackysack, doing tai chi in the mornings, and companies having pep rallies or gatherings.

Of course, weekends are the time for people watching, but weekdays are the time for more peace and quiet. Yes, we're still in Vietnam, so whenever there are people at Tao Dan, you'll encounter a lot of cigarette smoke and many amplified megaphones and blasting karaoke speakers. Sorry. But it's much quieter on weekdays.

While the park is open until 10 PM, after sunset it can be kind of dodgy. It's a known place for drug deals and general low-level criminal activity. After dark, Tao Dan is probably the easiest place in central Saigon to get mugged, if that's on your Vietnamese Adventure Travel Experience itinerary.

The funny thing is that many Vietnamese people recommend not going to Tao Dan after dark because it's supposedly haunted by ghosts. That's good advice, even if from the wrong reasoning. In daylight, including dawn, it's safe.

During the day, trees at Tao Dan provide shade from the sun, so it's possible to go even in the middle of the day, and still not get too terribly burned. And where there are trees, there are birds! You can see them and hear them. Vietnamese and foreign birdwatchers alike come with their cameras and binoculars.

About the birds: Some twenty years ago, the bird population at Tao Dan was nearly extinct, simply because Vietnam's widespread poverty forced people to catch and eat any birds they could find. Nowadays, there are many fewer hungry people in Saigon than there used to be — and the bird population at Tao Dan has been recovering! You can see and hear many beautiful songbirds, especially in the early mornings.

Other sources may send you to a corner of the park where supposedly old men gather with their pet birds every early morning. Unfortunately, those guys and their birds haven't been there for a good five years now. One lone old guy sitting around with his pet bird told me that the guys from that group all died off. (By the way, why do Saigonese men usually die in their sixties? Light a cigarette and think it over!)

Fashions go in cycles, so it's possible that a new generation of bird keepers may restart the tradition, but as of this writing, there is no bird group in the early mornings at Tao Dan.

Last thing: If you see Vietnamese people giggle at the mention of birds, it's because the word for a bird, *cu* or *con cu*, is also the usual Saigonese slang term for a penis. The more you know!

Neighborhood Buddhist temple

Vietnamese people are predominantly Buddhist, in some form or another. Generally, like many things in Vietnam, Buddhism is loosely construed and loosely enforced, and is not something people get too uptight about. Still, when someone has an important life moment, or just needs spiritual cleansing of some sort, a Vietnamese Buddhist will often visit a Buddhist temple.

I'm going to show you an interesting neighborhood temple that sees few if any tourists. And if you're expecting temples in Vietnam to be uptight places where you have to stay silent and follow a dress code (cough cough *Thailand* cough cough), we're a lot more easygoing than that.

This temple is called Chua On Lang or Chua Quan Am ("chua" means "temple" in Vietnamese). It's at 12 Lao Tu Street in Q5. Have you heard of the Chinese philosopher Lao Tzu? Lao Tu is the Vietnamese version of that name.

This temple was built in the 19th century by the Chinese traders of Cho Lon (now Q5/Q6), and places a strong emphasis on the sea – as the Chinese people in Vietnam are primarily known as seafaring people (in fact, one derogatory term for Chinese people in Vietnamese is to call them "boats"). It's the oldest temple in Saigon. Many people in Saigon have some Chinese ancestry, and this temple, although theoretically a "Chinese" temple, is popular even with people who have no Chinese ancestry.

Generally people come here to burn offerings to their ancestors, donate money, and pray for good fortune. It's similar to other Buddhist temples, although I like it for its neighborhood "working temple" feel; it feels less like a museum and more like a neighborhood gathering place, which is exactly what it is.

MY SAIGON: THE LOCAL GUIDE TO HO CHI MINH CITY, VIETNAM

Speaking of burning offerings to ancestors: some tourists and even some guidebooks refer to Saigonese people "burning garbage on the street." It's not garbage. They're actually burning paper offerings to send to their dead ancestors. You can buy fake money and even paper luxury cars to burn to send to your ancestors in the afterlife. Want Grandma to be cruising around the afterlife in a Bentley? A burnable paper Bentley is one of the most popular offerings to burn. Most people don't believe it as literal truth that their ancestors will receive those things, but it's done to show respect to their deceased ancestors.

Anyway, near this temple, vendors do sell paper offerings to send to one's ancestors (including paper Bentleys), as well as incense, birds to release for making merit, and various other Chinese buddhist artifacts – as well as the expected coffee, sugarcane juice, and snacks! And inside the temple itself, you'll find very good deals on small jade necklaces, generally selling for around 100,000 VND – the same jade necklaces being sold at Ben Thanh Market for over 1,000,000 VND. (Note: Do not negotiate prices at the temple! Please don't do that! Anyway, these prices are already really low.)

Dress code: don't look like a dirty backpacker, but there's nothing wrong with wearing shorts, t-shirts, or sandals, as long as you look modest and respectful. Approximate opening times: 9AM – 5PM every day.

I'm showing you a neighborhood place, so I'd like you to follow some neighborhood etiquette, lest the temple attendees and employees become unhappy with the tourists Elly is sending to them: it's polite to donate a small sum of money (say 10,000 – 20,000, though they certainly won't reject bigger amounts) to the collection box at the front. Don't touch monks

(I don't know why you'd want to do that, but that's always an explicitly stated prohibition). There's no hard ban on photography, but please don't aggressively take photos of people enjoying a private spiritual moment, and take it easy with the flash.

    Chua On Lang / Chua Quan Am
    12 Lao Tu
    Q5, P4

Saigon's Cao Dai temple: uniquely Vietnamese

Cao Dai is a South Vietnamese religion that started in 1926 in Tay Ninh, about 100 km from Saigon. Almost all its practitioners are ethnically Vietnamese (often outside of Vietnam, as Cao Dai was illegal in Vietnam from 1975 until 1997) – although British novelist Graham Greene did famously consider converting to Cao Dai.

Tour companies love to pitch you a tour to the Cao Dai temple in Tay Ninh, because they can charge you a hefty fee to take you about two hours out of town. What they don't want you to know is that there's a big Cao Dai temple right in Saigon! It's not as big as the one in Tay Ninh, but still, it's worth seeing – and unless you are extremely interested in Cao Dai, I think it might be a waste of a day (and of your money) to go all the way out to Tay Ninh to see the temple. (By the way, if you really do want to see the temple in Tay Ninh, you can just take a public bus there from central Saigon for something like 10,000 VND.)

Saigon's main Cao Dai temple is at 891 Tran Hung Dao, Q5, P1. The Vietnamese name for it is "Thanh that Cao Dai" (Cao Dai temple) or "Thanh that Sai Gon" (Saigon Temple). The temple is casually open all day, and you can walk in and take a look around. There's no English-language signage, but the people working there will welcome you in, and some of them might speak English.

I suggest you briefly research Cao Dai religion on Wikipedia or a similar resource before you go, just so you can better understand what you're seeing. One of the most important symbols of Cao Dai – and one you'll see throughout the temple – is the all-seeing eye, which symbolizes that God always watches over humanity. It's similar in appearance to the eye on the back of US dollars. You'll see many paintings of this eye.

The temple has services at noon and 6 PM. If there's no service when you visit, go around the temple, and especially go up to the highest levels and the steeples, accessible by narrow stairs (maybe not recommended if you're not in good physical condition). Much of the symbolism of Cao Dai relates to climbing and going upward ("cao" means tall or high in Vietnamese and Cantonese), and the temple also saves the best stuff for the highest floors.

There's no dress code, but please remove your shoes in the worship areas. There is a donation box at the ground floor, and it's polite to drop 10,000 VND or so into the box.

Hair wash

A Vietnamese pastime you might not know about: having your hair washed. It's even more popular than massage. And it's not a five-minute hair-washing. It usually takes about an hour, with multiple cycles of washing and rinsing and conditioning and so on. It also usually includes washing your face and massaging your neck, and sometimes even shaving all over your face (both men and women). It's great as a midday break on a hot day, and might be perfect for you if you've been walking around in the Saigon heat. Hair washing is equally popular for men and women, and sometimes husband and wife or boyfriend and girlfriend will go together for a hair wash.

Hair washing is called "goi dau." In the tourist area, "goi dau" has been taken over by the pretty-girl salons (described in this book) that seek to make tourists think there's something more than a hair wash. They're not that great for a hair wash, and are much too expensive.

For a good hair wash, you can go to any hair salon you see anywhere, and ask for "goi dau." I suggest you stay away from the salons immediately adjacent to Ben Thanh Market, because they are tourist traps, and might not give you a very good experience, and will certainly charge you a high price. The average price for a hair wash in Saigon nowadays is about 50,000 – 70,000 VND. You can also, optionally, tip about 20,000 – 50,000, to bring the total up to about 100,000. Not bad for an hour of fun!

There's one very good but very expensive salon I can recommend to you for goi dau (and in fact any hair services), right in the middle of the tourist area, but with almost no tourist clientele. The salon is called Hai, and it's at 169 Ly Tu Trong in Q1, near Ben Thanh market.

Unbeknownst to the tourists who stay in hotels nearby, Hai is where many Vietnamese celebrities and government officials have their hair done. In fact, celebrity-watching is considered part of the benefit of going to Hai.

Nothing is free, because Hai is super mega expensive. Not as expensive as the tourist ripoff places, but still, super expensive. They charge about three times the normal Saigon price for goi dau and for haircuts and the like. It is an excellent hair wash and an excellent haircut, but it's not exactly cheap. Expect to pay about 150,000 VND for a hair wash. It might still be worth it for you, as there are few good hair shops in the central tourist area, and you'd spend money on a taxi going to another one – and at least at Hai, the excellent service does match the high price.

Vietnamese green bean cakes

The previous section talked about Hai Salon, an excellent (but expensive) hair salon on Ly Tu Trong street in Q1. Right next to Hai Salon – and in fact, often a combined stop for is patrons – is Rong Vang, at 167 Ly Tu Trong, a shop selling pastries, dried meats, and its specialty, green bean cakes.

It's funny that tourists buy horrible-tasting, low-quality, wildly overpriced snacks and dried foods at Ben Thanh, but almost never know about Rong Vang, right in their hotel neighborhood! Well, like many successful businesses, Rong Vang doesn't advertise, especially not to tourists, because it's such a well-known shop (at least to Vietnamese people) that it has no shortage of business.

You can confidently buy things like candy and dried meat at Rong Vang to take back home, and it'll be a million times better than what you find at Ben Thanh market. But the specialty of Rong Vang is green bean cakes, called "banh dau xanh" and the cookies made from those cakes, "banh dau xanh nuong." Green bean cakes are ultra-sweet and meant to be eaten with bitter coffee or tea; they resemble Vietnamese baklava. They are a popular gift for Saigonese people to give and receive, and I suggest you consider getting these green bean cakes as a souvenir or as a gift! One box will cost about 25,000 VND for regular green bean cakes or about 35,000 for cookies ("banh nuong").

Where to meet university students

There's a park between the Ben Thanh Market area and Pham Ngu Lao. It's called 23-9 (or September 23) park. Because it's close to the main tourist hotspots, many Vietnamese university students, and their teachers, go to this park just for the novelty of chatting in English with foreigners. It sounds odd to just go somewhere to talk to strangers, but that's how hardworking we Vietnamese students are, and the lengths we'll go to to improve our conversational English.

If you go to 23-9 park most afternoons, say around 5 PM (but even any other time of day), you can find small groups of Vietnamese high school and university students who would love to chat in English. They are most commonly under the "gazebo" type roof coverings, huddled in small groups, and carrying notebooks around. You can just come up to a group and ask them whether they'd like to practice English. You can have fun talking about Vietnam and Vietnamese language, and maybe make new friends.

Even if you want a Vietnamese girlfriend (or boyfriend), remember that these students' primary purpose is to learn English from you, and if they're talking to you, that doesn't mean that they're attracted to you! In fact, often a boyfriend and girlfriend go on a date together to this park, to talk to foreigners together, as a date activity.

On the other hand, yes, sometimes you'll meet students who are single and interested in dating foreigners, but that really shouldn't be your purpose in going to this park. Unless you want to be considered a "goat." (That's Vietnamese slang for a pervert or dirty old man.)

Note that there is now an online group to facilitate meetings between Vietnamese students and foreign tourists in this park: see twtt.org (twtt stands for Talking With The Tourist). I don't know them personally, but just noticed them online.

You can bring a pen and notebook to the park, as most of the students have, for writing down newly learned Vietnamese, for illustrating English, and perhaps for writing down your new friends' contact details.

If you make new university-student friends at 23-9 park, don't unfriend me yet, because most university students in Saigon are not from Saigon. They don't know much about the city. So don't expect them to be experts on Saigon. But you can definitely enjoy hearing their perspectives!

Of course, the same caution applies in this park as when talking with strangers anywhere else in the world. Be careful with strangers. There are some scam artists around this park, as there would be in any meeting place anywhere in the world. There are "helpful tour guides" who will milk you for commissions and there will be "Vietnamese" (really Filipino) "professors" (really street thugs) who would love to take you to a "casino" down a back alley, after you just withdraw some cash from the ATM. There are also Amway and Herbalife recruiters! Oh no! But those are all extreme (although real) cases. Usually the most "dangerous" thing you might find at this park is an overly romantically aggressive man or woman... which is not exclusive to Saigon!

Where to listen to live music

Saigon has a hopping live music scene! In addition to hearing music, you can see real Saigonese nightlife, of both the younger and slightly older generations.

At all these places, the music starts around 8:30 P.M., and goes until about 11:00 P.M. or midnight. Drinks cost about 100,000-120,000 VND each, and there's no cover charge. One nice thing about bars and music venues in Vietnam is that they serve a good range of non-alcoholic drinks. You can usually order a sinh to (fruit shake) or a juice or an iced coffee in a late-night music venue, and no one will think you're strange. Maybe this is because of Vietnam's coffee culture, combined with the fact that traditionally, "proper" Vietnamese women don't drink alcohol.

A bit of an additional note: the music places I've listed here are some of the very few live music venues in Saigon where you can hear Vietnamese musicians. There's a common belief among Vietnamese music venue owners that Vietnamese people won't pay to hear music performed by Vietnamese people. The result is that many bars and other venues have a flat-out, firm policy of "no Vietnamese musicians allowed." That sounds ridiculous (and illegal) if it happened in most first-world countries, but it's just the way things are in Vietnam. But I think if you want to experience Saigon, you should experience some Vietnamese musicians. And all these venues – with the exception of Thi, which usually has Filipino musicians – feature Vietnamese musicians. Hooray!

<u>Acoustic</u>

6 Ngo Thoi Nhiem Street, Q3 (but very close to Q1)
facebook.com/acousticbarpage

This is the most famous place in Saigon for young people to listen to live music. They have live bands and pop singers every evening. Many of the singers are the same ones that sing on Vietnamese talent TV shows like Vietnam Idol. You can generally find pop singers singing Western songs, and quite a few foreigners hang out here. Generally the music goes from 9 PM until 11 PM. Warning: very crowded, sometimes literally can't move inside (what if there's a fire?!), rude staff who might push you out of the way if they think you're standing in the wrong place, and there is very thick cigarette smoke.

Main age group: 16-25

Yoko

22 Nguyen Thi Dieu Street, Q3 (but close to Q1)

This place is geographically very close to Acoustic, but it's smaller and more intimate. In its previous incarnation, it was a place for music nerds to hear more obscure music, but in 2014 it was sold to a new owner, who is making it just like Acoustic, with rotating pop singers.

Main age group: 20-40

Vung

17 Ngo Thoi Nhiem, Q1

https://vi-vn.facebook.com/V%E1%BB%ABng-%C6%A1i-m%E1%BB%9F-ra-Cafe-141160225904005/

Vung is on the same street as Acoustic, but it's very, very different. It's an intimate place with live piano-and-vocals music every night. No smoking. No yelling. No rowdiness. Hooray! Note that it's crowded, so you may have to wait a bit

MY SAIGON: THE LOCAL GUIDE TO HO CHI MINH CITY, VIETNAM

for a seat, or you can call for reservations. The manager speaks English.

<u>Thi</u>

224 De Tham Street, in Pham Ngu Lao, Q1

The music isn't very good, and there are lots of prostitutes hanging out, but there's also a good amount of cool Vietnamese university students and other people, and this place is open until 3AM and usually is not too expensive. The musicians are usually Filipino, and drunk tourists sometimes "help" them sing. Good Morning Vietnam, an Italian restaurant directly across the street from Thi, has pretty good pizzas!

Main age group: 25-35

Nhau (getting drunk)

When Vietnamese people, especially men, aren't hanging out in coffeeshops or getting hair washes and massages, what are they doing for fun? Maybe they're going out to "nhau." Nhau, pronounced "nyau," literally means "get together," but in Saigonese culture it means getting very drunk in a big group, at a bar specifically made for the purpose, a "quan nhau" (celebration house).

You can recognize a quan nhau by big groups (say, five or more) of predominantly men (but sometimes with their wives, girlfriends, or mistresses) sitting on small seats around a long table, with a lot of alcohol and some snacks on the table. The usual foods for nhau are dried squid (chewed like gum), hotpot, and snails.

One phrase foreigners in Saigon seem to have picked up on sounds like "mot hai ba, yo!" which is a drinking toast from the world of "nhau." On the last word of the toast, everyone is supposed to finish their drinks. It literally means "one two three, finish!"

Vietnamese people don't often have a glass of beer or wine with dinner. Vietnamese men's drinking is (unfortunately) more like what's called "binge drinking": occasionally drinking big quantities of alcohol, probably to the point of vomiting.

In general, "proper" Vietnamese women will always say that they don't drink, although some in reality do very much like to drink. Anyway, the "nhau" culture is very, very male-dominated. I've never heard of women going out to nhau, the way that Sex and the City women might go out for some wine. And the "nhau" culture is often mixed with ogling women and going out to prostitutes. Maybe it's a little bit like going to Hooters in the US!

So if you're a woman or a group of women, you won't be turned away from "nhau," but you'll probably feel more comfortable and endure less staring if you go with some men. Sorry, I didn't invent this Vietnamese sexism; I'm just reporting it to you.

Places for nhau, formal and informal, are all over Saigon. The ones in Q1 will have English menus, and you and your friends can try your hand at Vietnamese-style drinking if you'd like. Just be aware that nhau does attract riffraff, or sometimes rowdy behavior from otherwise non-riffraff, so be careful, especially with your phones!

One place for "nhau" right in the center of the tourist area, near Ben Thanh Market, is called Saigon Night, and it's at 35 Nguyen Trung Truc, near Ly Tu Trong Street (where I recommend you stay). It's safe and relatively upscale as a "nhau" establishment.

And the culture of "nhau" has extended to Vietnamese enclaves in the US, and almost any big US city is likely to have some "nhau" establishments, if you want to try this out before coming to Vietnam – although again I am warning you that "nhau" can attract some pretty rowdy people.

A Vietnamese massage you might not enjoy

I know that tourists love to get massages in Vietnam. For Vietnamese people, massages are divided into three pretty strict categories:

1) Massage for women, in a beauty shop or salon
2) Massage for men, with sexual services
3) Foot massage, gender neutral, nonsexual

To make things a bit more complicated, "foot massage" is just a name, but actually your whole body is massaged. It's just that you're in a room with other people, and wear maybe a t-shirt and shorts or a provided robe, and aren't completely nude.

Body massage for women is the rarest of the three. But it works pretty much as massage in the West works. You don't need my advice on it. You can find it in many beauty salons, or in female-oriented spas.

Body massage for men is really in the realm of prostitution, and something I won't cover in this book. If you speak Vietnamese, you can probably ask your male Vietnamese buddies about it. Otherwise, it is not offered anywhere in the tourist areas, because the Vietnamese government is very intent on not making Vietnam a destination for sex tourism. (By the way, if a woman attempts to go to a "body massage for men" establishment, she won't be welcome, just because she's unlikely to spend on the sexual services that are the real core of the business.)

So that leaves us with "foot massage" (which, again, is a massage of your whole body, starting with your feet), for men, women, anyone. It's the most common form of massage in Vietnam, and is a popular way for people to unwind.

There is one famous foot massage place in Saigon that I recommend. But you might not like it. It's a bit gritty. You enter an almost unmarked door on the street. Then you're led upstairs and you sit in big reclining chairs, with other people around, both men and women. Some other customers around you might be smoking or drinking or telling dirty jokes in Vietnamese. No one speaks English. And the massage is really hard and strong, and there's no "well-trained therapist" or balancing your chakras or any of that stuff that Westerners often like. It's just a really great, really strong massage. There's a steam bucket to heat up your feet, and the massage focuses on your feet, but will be all over your body, including even massaging your face at the end.

Here are the good points: this is where my friends and I would go for a massage. It's a real Vietnamese place. The massage feels wonderful, and it's super-strong. And the price is 120,000 VND (about $5 USD) for a ninety-minute massage, including a (non-alcoholic) drink.

You *must* tip at any Vietnamese massage shop. In most places in Vietnam, tipping is uncommon. But in massage places, tipping is mandatory. And it's not the 15% tipping common in the US. An average tip at a place like this is about 100% of the basic fee, so about 120,000 VND. Keep in mind that the massage girls don't make any salary (technically, they make minimum wage, about 1.5 million VND per month, which is then deducted down to zero for "expenses" like

MY SAIGON: THE LOCAL GUIDE TO HO CHI MINH CITY, VIETNAM

uniforms and massage lotion), and depend only on tips – and sometimes wait all day for one customer. The smallest tip that won't get swear words yelled at you is probably 100,000 VND. A mildly generous (not huge) tip is 200,000 VND. Vietnamese bigshots routinely tip 500,000 VND at places like this – and yes, only for a massage. (By the way, there are no sexual services here, though I'm sure many of the massage girls wouldn't mind dating a foreigner!) A good rule of thumb for tipping at a Vietnamese massage shop is that a 150,000 tip is like a 15% tip in the US, a 200,000 tip is like a 20% tip in the US, and so on.

So here's how it works. Walk in. Say you want a foot massage (in English is ok). You can pay your 120,000 massage fee right away at the front desk, or pay later after you finish. If you want, you can stop off at the changing room to put on their supplied robe and shorts, or just wear your regular street clothes if they're comfortable enough. You can also shower in the changing room downstairs. They'll take you upstairs and sit you in a big soft chair. Yes, a big recliner chair, not a table. Don't get naked!

You can order a drink – usually coffee or a soda or tea or water. Then a massage girl will come and massage you, and the waiter will come and bring your drink and snacks. (You don't have to tip the waiter, but if you want, you can tip him about 10,000 VND.)

Start the massage lying face-up, and after about one hour, the massage girl will tell you to lie down, and if you want her to use oil ("dau," pronounced "yau") on your back, to take off your shirt. There are showers downstairs in the changing room, so if she uses oil, you can wash it off later if you want.

ELLY THUY NGUYEN

Have fun, but don't go here unless you're sure you'll enjoy a real, strong local Vietnamese massage, because many foreigners don't enjoy this place at all.
Khang Lac Massage
452 Tran Hung Dao, Q5
noon – midnight
phone 08-39236970

Moshi moshi, Japantown

If you want to see something different, there's a Japantown area – for Japanese tourists and also young Vietnamese hipsters – very close to Ben Thanh Market and the central city. The area doesn't have an official name, but the address you should go to is 8 Le Thanh Ton Street, Q1. At this address is a small alley (a "hem" in Vietnamese). The alley is T shaped. Go straight, and then left or right, and you will find many small Japanese restaurants, massage shops, souvenir shops, and cafes, in an architectural style that resembles traditional Japan. It's a cute area, and you can get some good Japanese food (especially my favorite, ramen!), and take a break from the usual Vietnamese stuff. And it's quite popular with younger Vietnamese people, especially university students and young IT workers from the companies nearby, so it is really more of a local hangout than a Japanese tourist hangout, although Japanese tourists are the original target market.

Clothes shopping

Tourists love to go to Ben Thanh Market. It used to be a real Vietnamese market, but nowadays it's really a big tourist gift shop. That's still ok, because gift shops can still have some things you want to buy, but nowadays, really, other than some food stalls, Ben Thanh Market just consists of the same vendors selling the same overpriced China-made trinkets to tourists, over and over and over.

Don't buy anything at Ben Thanh Market if you can't immediately inspect its quality, because the sellers at Ben Thanh are mostly set up for tourists, and they know that tourists won't open the package and inspect the goods until they're back in their home countries – and too far away to complain.

So I'm going to give you four alternatives to Ben Thanh Market for clothes shopping, other than the supermarkets I mentioned earlier (which do sell clothes!).

Usual caveat applies: if you weigh more than about 70 kg = 150 lbs for women, or 100 kg = 220 lbs for men, you are very unlikely to find any clothes in Saigon that fit you. If you really do need big-size clothes, search for "big size" on Google Maps (the "big and tall" stores here are literally called "Big Size"), or shop online on Lazada.

Anyway, assuming you're the size of an average Vietnamese person, here's where to buy clothes:

1. Van Hanh Mall, 11 Su Van Hanh in Q10 (really not that far from the central city). This is the main clothes shopping mall and has many reasonably priced clothes at fixed prices. No

bargaining, no rude in-your-face vendors, no pickpockets — imagine!

2. Nguyen Trai Street, which goes from the Ben Thanh area into Q5, is full of small clothing shops. This is mostly fashion clothing for women, not stuff like souvenir t-shirts and trinkets.

3. Saigon Square 1 and Saigon Square 2 are two big clothing malls, with lots of small sellers selling young people's fashion. Yes, you have to bargain, but usually it's cheaper and higher-quality than Ben Thanh Market. Saigon Square 1 and 2 are pretty equivalent in size and quality, so it's really a tossup as to which one you go to. One is at 77 Nam Ky Khoi Nghia Street, near the intersection with Pasteur Street, and the other one is at 7 Ton Duc Thang Street near the Saigon River.

4. An Dong Plaza (18 An Duong Vuong Street, Q5) is a bigger and cheaper mall, similar to Saigon Square, in Q5, not far from Q1. It might be your adventurous choice. And as with the other places, it's mostly set up for young women's fashion – so this is the kind of place I know about, but maybe it doesn't interest you if you're not a twentysomething girl like me.

Don't overpay for luggage

Somehow most visitors to Vietnam end up needing to buy more luggage to accommodate all the random stuff they bought here. And the vendors at Ben Thanh Market and the tourist area surrounding it know that very well. The initial price they quote you for their luggage is about ten times what we Vietnamese people pay, without bargaining, at a regular store.

There's a street in central Saigon that's famous (among Vietnamese people) for selling luggage. It's called Cach Mang Thang Tam, or CMT8.

The street starts near the Starbucks at the New World Hotel, and extends all the way out to Tan Binh, near the airport. If you want to pay a bit more — but not nearly as much as tourist prices — there's a luggage store called Mai right at that Starbucks traffic circle. Mai is fine, but they have about a 50% markup over less nicely decorated stores farther down CMT8.

The luggage store I and many in-the-know people recommend is Van Phuc (stop giggling), at 1158 CMT8 in Tan Binh. See their website: https://balovanphuc.com/

Van Phuc looks like a giant storeroom of every kind of luggage. As far as I know, there's no bargaining, and you just walk in and choose and pay.

To give you an idea, I just went there the other day to buy a basic 20" (yes, we measure suitcases in inches) hardsided roller suitcase, and I paid 300K VND ($13). That suitcase costs 600K at Mai in the center in the city, and has an opening price of 1.1 million at Ben Thanh Market.

If you want to try a store other than Van Phuc, then the magic word to look for in Google Maps and on store signs is *vali or va li* (from the French *valise*), which is a suitcase in Vietnamese.

Oh, what does Cach Mang Thang Tam mean? It means August Revolution. In August 1945, the Viet Minh were able to seize most of North Vietnam and some of South Vietnam from Vietnam's Japanese colonial rulers. Or, according to the official history, the Communists seized all of Vietnam from Vietnam's French colonial rulers. (Just like the official history that on April 30, 1975, the Communists won against the American military — despite the American military having left Vietnam in 1973.)

Medical tourism

It's one of the most common questions asked by potential visitors: *Can I get medical stuff done in Saigon?*

You know my answer: *You can, but may you?*

Seriously though, you can, but you have to be more careful than you'd be in the first world. There are excellent physicians, dentists, and optometrists in Vietnam, just as there are in your country.

But due to us being a "developing economy," there are many, many more outright dangerous quacks and incompetents out there — and unlike in your country, there's no functioning medical licensing board or tort law system (Well technically, we do have both of those in Vietnam, but you know...).

So if you choose your doctor poorly in Vietnam, the consequences can be seriously bad, and quite a few medical tourists die or experience serious complications because they went to substandard medical providers.

Note that a shiny office, well-produced YouTube ads, and English-speaking receptionists are no guarantee of a good place. All it means is they have capital and business sense.

This is a big topic, but in brief, in Vietnam, it's easy to buy an MD diploma without ever attending medical school. It costs around $50,000, which you can make back pretty quickly. The top few medical schools in Vietnam don't sell diplomas (at least as far as my doctor friends tell me), but the dozens of non-elite medical schools fund themselves by selling diplomas.

Then there is the common practice in Vietnam of one physician "renting out" their license to someone else, or a few someone elses. Dr. Quack Doc Nguyen might have a medical diploma (however it may have been obtained), but the person working on you might not be the real Dr. Quack Doc Nguyen, but someone paying to rent their diploma and license.

Especially in cosmetic surgery, many of the shiny clinics along major streets are run by very questionable "doctors," some of whom admit (in private company, to my doctor friends) that they never actually attended medical school, and learned their trade on YouTube, or sometimes by watching a real doctor work.

Also, we Vietnamese people just love going to "foreign" doctors, usually from the US or Korea, who are working in Vietnam. A large fraction of these foreign doctors are working in Vietnam because they lost their medical licenses (or faced other disrepute) back in their home countries. According to my physician dad, a US investigative journalist found that more than half of the American doctors in Vietnam had lost their licenses back in the US for misconduct before coming here. Think about it: If you were a doctor in the US, why would you take a huge pay cut and go work in Vietnam unless it was your only option?

Additionally, in Vietnam's public hospitals, hygiene standards are shockingly bad, and "diagnoses" and "treatments" are done in literally a minute or two, to move on to the next patient — that is how we are able to offer medical care in public hospitals for around $5 a visit. It's better than jungle medicine, but it's probably not what you're looking for.

MY SAIGON: THE LOCAL GUIDE TO HO CHI MINH CITY, VIETNAM

Also, doctors in public hospitals usually solicit bribes or additional payments, especially from foreigners. And they are very likely to follow the treatment path that yields them the most money — often recommending "medical devices" or "medicine" from businesses they own.

Now that I've scared you about quacks, public hospitals, and disgraced foreign doctors, here's the absolutely good news: There are great, reputable clinics and doctors here.

Your starting point should be FV Hospital in Quan 7. (Note that they have a second location in Quan 1, which has fewer services and higher prices.) FV Hospital is as trustworthy as you can get in Vietnam. As in the US, you're not 100% guaranteed an excellent outcome, but it's pretty close.

They have everything from emergency treatment to cosmetic surgery to psychiatric care to cancer treatment. Prices are much higher than in a "regular" Vietnamese hospital, but still much lower than in the US. Expect to pay about $30 for a regular doctor's visit, and about an additional $30 if you want some small procedure. Of course, those are estimates. Get more info by emailing information@fvhospital.com

For dentistry, go to Nha Khoa Minh Khai (*nha khoa* means *dentist*): https://nhakhoaminhkhai.net/ They are great and they speak English.

On the other hand, there are a few "international dentists" around town, especially near Ben Thanh Market, and they are the dental equivalent of tourist traps. Avoid.

Lastly, eyeglasses. I've heard how much prescription eyeglasses cost in the US. Yikes. You can get a prescription for something like $3 (really) and get eyeglasses, depending on which frames you want, for as little as $10 (or much more if you want more fashionable frames, higher end materials, etc).

Fun fact: We Vietnamese (cough cough, Southern Chinese) people are genetically predisposed to needing eyeglasses. It's unfortunately not because we're so smart. It's genetics. So the eyeglass market is hugely competitive.

The most famous place is Saigon Optic, aka Mat Kinh Saigon. It's on Pham Ngoc Thach, very close to Turtle Lake (Ho Con Rua): https://saigonoptic.com.vn/ . Note that this place is ruthlessly copied, and there are dozens of fakes around town, so make sure you go to the real one. However, the problem with Saigon Optic / Mat Kinh Saigon is that they don't speak any English. And I've heard that they're pretty impatient with non-Vietnamese-speaking customers, because they're a busy place and don't have time to explain and translate for you.

So I have another very reputable and fluently English-speaking recommendation for eyeglasses: Nguyen Optical. Nguyen Optical is a small, family-run business. They speak fluent English and specialize in Viet Kieu (Vietnamese American) customers. Tons of Vietnamese Americans have Nguyen Optic make their eyeglasses, either during their visits to Saigon, or by mail to the US. As with every business I recommend, I have no affiliation with them, and they don't know that they'll be in this guidebook. I just know they're good.

They work by appointment only, so contact them on Facebook at Tiem Mat Kinh Nguyen. Use the QR code for their Facebook:

MY SAIGON: THE LOCAL GUIDE TO HO CHI MINH CITY, VIETNAM

Chuc ban khoe! (I wish you good health!)

Taxi scams

Every country has taxi scams. In Saigon, taxi scams are the most common scams encountered by tourists. We have a few different levels of taxi scams. The most benign is that the driver will take a slightly longer route – like almost any taxi driver almost anywhere in the world! A little bit less benign is when the meter is manipulated, and runs very quickly. And the worst kind is when the driver suddenly locks the doors and demands $100 USD if you want to be let out, and threatens to beat you up or take you to his friends who will beat you up.

The good news is that dishonest taxi drivers are a very very small minority of Saigon taxi drivers. But the bad news is that the dishonest taxi drivers are the ones who most seek out tourists. So while an average Vietnamese person might only very rarely encounter dishonest taxi drivers, you, as a tourist, might encounter them quite often! Hey, remember that in any country, the worst kind of scammers are attracted to the tourist areas; taxis are no different.

The other good news is that even if the meter runs fast, the amount you'll pay for the taxi is still probably less than what you'd pay in your home country. You might be cheated for something like $20 USD (500,000 Vietnamese dong), which is a huge cheat in Vietnam, and a big amount of money for a taxi driver, but I think that if you can afford a plane ticket to Vietnam, losing $20 will not completely ruin your lifetime finances!

And the last good news is that while those taxi drivers in the third category will talk big and threatening, they will never actually harm you. The laws in Vietnam, especially for harming foreigners, are tough.

If you ever encounter a taxi driver in the third category, who locks you in the back seat and demands some big amount of money in order to let you out, my advice is calmly refuse to give him anything more than the real fare, and do your best to make a big scene and yell and scream in English and beat on the windows. Call the police (113) on your mobile phone. If you have something like an umbrella, start trying to break the taxi's windows. (By the way, these bad taxis almost always have dark tinted windows, just so it's hard for bystanders to see you yelling and waving inside.) The driver will back down. And no matter what the driver says, the police will take your side in any such dispute. The police does not tolerate violent threats against foreigners – not because the police is so nice, but because such threats seriously hurt Vietnam's reputation as a tourist and investment destination.

I've told you what to do if it happens to you, but unless you're on a strange masochistic urban-adventure kick, it's even better not to ever encounter any of these bad taxi situations, right?! So there's a very, very simple way to guarantee that you'll never encounter a driver from category 2 or 3 and will only rarely encounter a driver from category 1 (one who takes a slightly longer router to increase your fare by maybe $0.50 USD, as might happen anywhere in the world). If you follow my simple tip, you will be safe from taxi scams in Vietnam. I'm serious.

This is the simple tip: **TAKE ONLY TAXIS FROM THE COMPANY "VINASUN" THAT HAVE "VINASUN" WRITTEN ON THEM.**

MY SAIGON: THE LOCAL GUIDE TO HO CHI MINH CITY, VIETNAM

That's it. That's the simple tip. Vinasun is the biggest taxi company in Vietnam, and their drivers are pretty honest. Of course, there are many non-Vinasun drivers who are honest too. But Vinasun is so huge that you will never be inconvenienced by waiting for a Vinasun taxi.

And just remembering what Vinasun taxis look like, and only taking them, is a lot easier and more practical than if I wrote many pages about various shades of good and bad in the twenty or so different taxi companies operating in Saigon! It's easier to remember the simple rule: only take Vinasun taxis! By the way, the area immediately around Ben Thanh market is the headquarters of ripoff taxis in Saigon. Most other tourist attractions in Saigon also have them, especially in Q1 and Pham Ngu Lao, but ripoff taxis are very rare outside the main tourist areas.

Another quick and simple tip: any Korean-made car (Daewoo, Hyundai, etc) is a ripoff taxi. The good taxi companies always use Toyota cars. Some of the bad taxi companies also use Toyota cars – so not every Toyota is a good taxi, but every Korean car is a bad taxi.

There's a little bump in the road. Just a small one. Bad taxi drivers know that smart tourists have been told, or learned on their own, to only trust Vinasun taxis. So the dishonest taxi drivers often paint their cars to look similar to Vinasun taxis. And often they write things like "Vinasum" or "Vinasu" or "Vinaxun" on their taxis, to confuse tourists. Or sometimes the driver even somehow manages to get a Vinasun uniform that he wears, and when he tries to persuade you into his taxi, he shows you his Vinasun uniform, even though his car doesn't say Vinasun (which would be kind of like someone convincing you that they're a real police officer by showing you their big black boots!).

You can download the Vinasun app and use it to request a taxi. Yes, pay in cash, and you don't need anything other than your phone number to register on the app. Unfortunately, requesting a taxi on the Vinasun app is a bit like requesting a taxi anywhere else in the world: the drivers, even if they "accepted your request," come only if they feel like it. If there's a taxi on the street, you're better off getting one.

And the best option of all: use Grab, Vietnam's ride-hailing service. They're generally cheaper and better than any taxi, and give you a fixed price up-front. Yes, you can use them to and from the airport too. Download the Grab app before you come to Vietnam.

Shady business scams

A very good portion of the people who are cheated in Saigon are cheated because they took up the offer of prostitutes or cocaine or quick money – it doesn't justify them being cheated, but it does say that if you look for bad things, bad things will find you.

Here is one example of a very common scam in Vietnam. This one is usually run by Filipinos who claim to be Vietnamese, but it can be run by anyone, and it has many variations.

A man approaches you on the street and starts talking to you and asking you where you're from. Whatever place you say, he will say that he has a supermodel sister (if you're male) or a movie-star brother (if you're female) who's traveling to your hometown next week, and could you possibly meet with them and give them some tips on the place? Now you can see the attraction for the regular tourist: wow, a beautiful or handsome Vietnamese person is coming to my hometown, and I'll be their local contact!

So they invite you to their home, and once you're there, the beautiful/handsome sibling or niece is "on the way over" and never shows up. But while you are waiting, you are invited to some kind of card game or other gambling. You're told that you can make big money during this game. Sometimes they press you to go to an ATM so you can withdraw more cash to gamble, so that you can "earn more money" on their "sure thing" gambling game.

Well, you can guess how it ends. One way or another, they make you lose all your money. And maybe a fake policeman comes and demands a bribe or else he'll jail you for illegal gambling. And then they send you home, and remind you that if you tell the police about any of this, you'll be the one in trouble.

That's just one of the scams. The general rule is that you should not be attracted by these kinds of "opportunities" that come up on the streets of Saigon. They're scams.

Broken phone or laptop? Fret not!

If you have hardware mishaps with your phone or laptop, Vietnam has some excellent repair shops. Because of low labor prices and high hardware prices, electronics that would be discarded in other countries are repaired to like-new condition in Vietnam. The problem, however, is that repair shops that target tourists tend to be unethical, as they know that you'll be gone in a few days, and likely won't be complaining about them on Vietnamese-language technology forums.

Here are two repair shops that are absolutely skilled and absolutely trustworthy. If they cheat you, I will mail you one of my fingers, your choice. Ok, maybe I won't mail you a digit, but I promise that these shops won't cheat you, and I promise I have no affiliation with them, other than being their customer. Neither is accustomed to tourists, but their English is sufficient for discussing your electronics repair.

For phone repair:
Hung Dung Mobile
59 Hung Vuong
(near the Equatorial Hotel)
Quan 5, Phuong 4
+84 62733755
For laptop repair:
Long Binh
50 Nguyen Cu Trinh
(across the street from the Pullman Hotel)
Quan 1

ELLY THUY NGUYEN

longbinh.com.vn
+84 838360699

Don't wear that silly hat: cultural tips

You can wear whatever you want in Saigon (not so in Hanoi). If you wear shorts and a t-shirt to a restaurant or nightclub, it's generally ok, unless it's the fanciest sort of restaurant or nightclub. You can even wear shorts and flip-flops to a temple, unlike the case in Thailand. Saigon is a pretty laid-back place. But here I want to talk about what tourists often wear around Saigon.

Item 1 that tourists love to wear around Saigon: the "non la" conical hat, commonly worn in Vietnam's rice paddies. But what I want to tell you is that to us Vietnamese people, it looks ridiculous on anyone who is not actually working on a rice paddy! It is worn only by people from rural Vietnam, and it is a marker of a highly disadvantaged social position. It's a bit of a mark of shame. It's like having a "red neck" ("being a redneck") in America.

Other than rural peasants who are obviously rural peasants, no Vietnamese person in Saigon would want to be seen in one. And it looks completely ridiculous, to us Vietnamese people, on anyone who is not a rice paddy farmer. (I guess that's another shattered stereotype about Vietnam! Hey, we don't all wear "non la" conical hats around Saigon! And guess what, in Dubai, investment bankers don't ride around town on camels!)

Let me say again: you are free to wear whatever you want. Don't think I'm trying to restrict you. I'm only telling you what Saigonese people will think of you. If you wear that hat around Saigon, you will look like a tourist riding around an office park in Dubai on a camel. Or a tourist riding around Houston on horseback, in full cowboy gear. You can do it if you want, and no one will stop you, but I want you to know that Saigonese people will think you look ridiculous!

The other item that tourists are "tone deaf" about is a bit touchy to talk about. But here it is. Tourists in Saigon love to wear t-shirts and other paraphernalia with pictures of Ho Chi Minh, the current official flag of Vietnam (formerly the flag of North Vietnam), or the hammer and sickle symbol of the Communist Party. Well, I'm telling you that Vietnamese people, at least in Saigon, would never buy or wear that stuff, because it is a very, very sensitive subject. Are you catching my drift?

And that leads me to the other cultural tip that is even more touchy to talk about. Many tourists come to Saigon and want to talk to strangers about the Vietnam War in terms of "It was Vietnam against America and you guys won." It's a big topic, better suited for a history book than a tourist guidebook, but my advice to you here is not to make big blanket statements about the war, especially in Saigon, and especially when people in Saigon aren't at ease discussing these things if they want to stay out of jail. It's all a very, very sensitive subject. Ok? Ok.

The next point is more lighthearted. Guys. Guys, listen! When you go around Saigon with your Vietnamese prostitute "girlfriend," Vietnamese people all know what her job is and how you met her. Maybe you don't care, and that's cool, because you should hang out with whoever you like! But if you're shocked that Vietnamese people would guess that your "teacher" girlfriend is not really a teacher, don't be shocked. Vietnamese people know Vietnamese people. And often, as the

MY SAIGON: THE LOCAL GUIDE TO HO CHI MINH CITY, VIETNAM

story goes, they have seen the same woman with ten different foreign men in the past week!

Rightly or wrongly, prostitutes are shunned by Vietnamese society. And if you bring a prostitute or an ex-prostitute or a woman (or man) who seems to be a prostitute to a Vietnamese social function, you likely won't be invited again.

Elly's public service announcement

Here is an important rule of Saigon: Never give money to beggars, at least in the tourist areas. Never believe what child beggars tell you. Never buy things (like food or books or medicine) that child beggars ask you to buy for them. Never support or give money or even food or drinks to child street performers.

Why? Because it's all fake, and it's all controlled by the mafia. The poor people on the street don't get any of the money. The mafia takes it all. These people are enslaved by very powerful organized crime groups.

You've heard that slavery still exists in the 21st century, right? Well, here it is.

Your hotel and taxi driver are too scared to tell you this, because they'd get payback from the mafia if they warned you. But when, for example, a little boy on the street starts up a conversation with you in English, and asks you to buy baby formula for his baby sister, or a textbook for him, or medicine for his sick mom – he is doing the shopping for his mafia handler, who later resells the goods that tourists buy for that boy.

Nguyen Hue, Pham Ngu Lao, and other pedestrian areas are full of child performers, often "fire breathers." Encouraging them or giving them money supports and encourages child abuse, human trafficking, and slavery. Don't even give them a candy bar or a drink, because they are under strict orders to turn all that in to their mafia handlers for later resale.

It's too sad to talk about much in a fun guidebook, but we Vietnamese people are frustrated when we see tourists falling for the mafia's tricks, and handing over their money to the mafia, or thinking that food or medicine they are buying for a child on the street is going to needy children.

We are too scared to talk about it to you in person, but I'm writing this in a book, so I can be honest with you. All the beggars, especially the child beggars, in the tourist areas of Saigon are enslaved by a human trafficking mafia.

They are sometimes orphans or children of very poor parents from Vietnam's north and central highlands, or from Laos or Cambodia, and their parents sold them for a one-time cash payment from the mafia, and a promise of a better life for them in Saigon. The mafia teaches them English, and teaches them exactly what to say to tug on tourists' heartstrings. I hope you don't fall for it.

Why doesn't the Vietnamese government stop it? I'll let you figure that out.

If you want to really help disadvantaged Vietnamese kids, give a good tip to your hotel maid or waitress or Grab driver, because they are almost always supporting a few kids back in their home villages. Make sure to put the money in the employee's hand, preferably out of sight of the boss, because Vietnamese bosses generally confiscate any tips they can get their hands on. (Welcome to Workers' Paradise!)

On a similar note, there are now "non profit organizations" in Saigon collecting donations from tourists, purportedly for causes such as helping needy children or disaster victims or animals in Vietnam. Be extremely skeptical about where the donations go, even if someone claims to be collecting for a

MY SAIGON: THE LOCAL GUIDE TO HO CHI MINH CITY, VIETNAM

reputable organization such as Unicef, or even if the "non profit organization" has a nice big building and lots of ads, or collection boxes at the airport. Anyone can print themselves a badge that says *Unicef*. The money is not going where they say it's going.

The same goes for college students, usually in groups, who stop you on the street asking for donations or asking you to buy some trinkets to help a charity. No matter how nice the college students sound (hey, it's a sales job), the money will not go where they claim it will go. Definitely if they're collecting in a tourist area, the mafia at the very least has to get a big cut.

As advised above, it's much better to directly give a big tip to your waiter, your hotel room cleaner, or your sandwich vendor, instead of supporting an "organization" that hits up tourists for donations.

Elly rant over. Thanks for listening.

Send-off

Hey, have fun in my home city! I love Saigon, and I hope you'll love it too. I hope this guide is useful for you in your Saigon adventures. Di choi di! (Go have fun!)
 -Elly

Also by Elly Thuy Nguyen

My Saigon
My Saigon: The Local Guide to Ho Chi Minh City, Vietnam
Secrets to Live in Vietnam on $500 a Month
Da Nang and Hoi An, Vietnam
Dating Vietnamese Women
Happy in Hanoi: The Local Guide to Hanoi, Vietnam
Undiscovered Quy Nhon: The Local Guide to Vietnam's Beach Paradise

About the Author

Elly Thuy Nguyen is a devoted Saigon nerd. Saigon is her major hobby. Reading and writing are her other hobbies, and also her vocation: in her day job, Elly is an English-language marketing writer. In addition to her love of Saigon and the written word, Elly enjoys cafes, cats, hip-hop, and international travel.

Made in United States
North Haven, CT
12 February 2024